A Foretaste of Glory Divine

Stories from a Woman Destined for Greatness

Lady Jane Lowder

A Foretaste of Glory Divine
Copyright © 2013 by Sarah Jane Lowder
ALL RIGHTS RESERVED

All Scripture references are from the Authorized King James Version of the Bible.

McDougal Publishing is a ministry of The McDougal Foundation, Inc., a Maryland nonprofit corporation dedicated to spreading the Gospel of the Lord Jesus Christ to as many people as possible in the shortest time possible.

Published by:

McDougal Publishing
P.O. Box 3595
Hagerstown, MD 21742-3595
www.mcdougalpublishing.com

ISBN 978-1-58158-179-9

Printed in the United States of America
For Worldwide Distribution

Dedication

I dedicate this book to the memory of my beloved mother, Lillie Bee (Biles) Lowder (1911-1996). She always had a song in her heart, regardless of the situation.

The seven of us with Momma

Acknowledgments

My thanks to Helen Whitehead and others who patiently listened to many hours of my messages and took out the stories to be shared with people all over the world. They have a share in the reward.

My thanks to Harold McDougal for helping me put the stories together in a meaningful way.

My thanks to Diane McDougal and McDougal Publishing for making this volume possible.

Contents

Writing a Book? 7

Foreword by Harold McDougal 9

Part 1: Introductory Stories 11

Part 2: Stories from My Childhood 25

Part 3: Stories about Being Newly Saved 43

Part 4: Early Stories from Camp 53

Part 5: Missionary Stories 127

Part 6: Stories about Visions 221

Part 7: Stories about My Mom and Dad 257

Foretaste: *"a partial experience, knowledge, or taste of something to come in the future; anticipation."*

— Random House Dictionary

Writing a Book?

As far back as the 1970s, Brother Wallace Heflin, Jr. prophesied over me that I would one day write a book. Then, in the early 1980s, Jack and Pattie Chappell prophesied the same thing over me. And they were not the last ones to give me such a prophecy. Others prophesied the very same thing. I didn't know what to think about all these prophecies because I didn't think I had the ability to write a book. My excuse to God was that I couldn't even write a letter. How would I ever write a book?

The result was that I just dismissed the idea, and today I have to say that I'm not proud of that fact. It is terrible how we limit ourselves by fear of not being able to do something.

Before Sister Ruth Heflin died, she spoke to Brother Harold McDougal one day. He had helped her put together her own wonderful books. "Sister Jane will never write a book unless you take the time to go through her tapes," she told him, "take out all of those wonderful stories, and put them together and then bring her the finished manuscript." And that's how my first book, *High and Lifted Up*, got written. How wonderful! He told me there had been enough material for several books. I found it difficult to fathom then, and I can still hardly believe it.

Now, the Lord has done it again. Someone sat and listened to dozens of hours of my teachings, took out the stories from them, and sent them to Brother McDougal to be organized into a book. Thank God for their efforts. So here you have it: *A Foretaste of Glory Divine*.

Jane Lowder
Ashland, Virginia

Foreword by Harold McDougal

Those who have been blessed through the years to sit under the ministry of Lady Jane Lowder will love these stories culled from her sermons delivered over a period of many years at Calvary Campground in Ashland, Virginia. The stories are timeless and meaningful to each and every one of us.

It has been my privilege to edit the material for this classic volume. I have changed as little as possible so that the pure Jane Lowder can shine through. She is a unique individual, and those of us who know her count it a privilege. May the whole world know her through her books.

Those who have read her first book, *High and Lifted Up*, will recognize some stories, but most of them are new, and the context of the older stories is different this time around. Some stories overlap and repeat some small detail, but, again, it is in a different context.

Some suggested adding scripture verses or otherwise meaningful phrases to the text, but I felt that anything at all would only detract from the simplicity and beauty of the pure text as it came from Lady Jane's heart. After reading the book, I'm sure you will agree.

When she refers to "here," keep in mind that she was speaking from Calvary Campground in Ashland, Virginia.

Harold McDougal

Part 1

Introductory Stories

Singing through Tragedy

TRAGEDY CAN STRIKE WHEN YOU least expect it. I know this from experience. It happened to us on the farm when I was still a young girl.

If you bring in hay, and it is not as dried as it needs to be, and you put it in the barn like that, spontaneous combustion can occur, the hay will burn, and the resulting fire just might wipe out everything you have. That's what happened to us.

The blaze from the hay burned down the barn, and that was enough to push us into poverty. Just the year before, our dad, at the age of forty, had suffered a stroke, which left him paralyzed so that he could no longer work, and now the barn had burned down on top of that.

We had lived from that farm, milking thirty-three cows twice a day and selling the milk to the Carnation plant.

We still had lots of food in the pantry because we grew it, and then we canned it. So that's what we ate. We made our own soap, and we made our own lard. In fact, we made everything we used and grew everything we ate, so we never had to go to a grocery store.

But now that the barn had burned, the man who owned it was forced to sell his cows, and all of our cash income evaporated overnight. Now our family of nine, seven children and a father who could not work, faced a bleak future. And yet, as I think back on it, I don't remember ever hearing my mother complain. In fact, what I do remember is hearing her singing every single day.

Mom began her singing early in the morning: *"Blessed assurance, Jesus is mine. Oh, what a foretaste of glory divine."* She sang, *"What a friend we have in Jesus, all our sins and griefs to bare! What a privilege to carry everything to God in prayer."* It was four in the morning, and Mom was working at the old cook stove, making milk gravy for our breakfast. As she worked, she sang, *"We'll understand it better by and by."*

Later, when we were all out in the fields working, Momma could be heard singing as she worked the rows, *"Amazing grace, how sweet the sound that saved a wretch like me! I once was lost, but now I'm found. Was blind but now I see."*

A Foretaste of Glory Divine

We could hear her singing in the barnyard or in the chicken house. We could hear her singing anywhere she was, because that's what Mom did. She refused to be discouraged and, so, whatever happened, she kept singing to the Lord.

We children had not yet learned to be so happy about tragedy, and so this was not an easy time for any of us. Our family now went on Welfare, we wore cardboard in our shoes, and got free lunches at school, and we hated every moment of it.

I personally hated being on Welfare so much that there came a day when I said in my heart, "If I can ever get out from under this, I will never receive anything free again. If I can somehow get a job and start earning my own way in life, I will never again have to receive a handout from others." And that was my goal.

But things got a lot worse before they began to get better. We went from zero to less than zero. We had arrived, it seemed, to the pit of despair. Through this very dark period, Mom was still singing, but we children sometimes felt bitterness, disappointment, and discouragement. Mom did all she could to implant deep within each of us a hope, a vision, an expectation that we would somehow make it, that we would come out of this and be able to climb to higher heights. We would survive and not have to live our entire lives in this demeaning way.

As a young teenager, I still couldn't do much about our situation, but by the time I was fifteen, I had found a job washing dishes in a restaurant (at thirty-three cents an hour). That seemed like thirty-three dollars to me at the time. I had to start somewhere. My goal was to be the best dishwasher that restaurant had ever had, and I would never give my bosses any reason to fire me. Now, these many years later, they will still tell you that I was the best they'd ever had.

I went from dishwasher to curb hopping, from curb hopping to short-order grilling, and from short-order grilling to being a waitress and serving lunch, from being a waitress to going in and cooking and preparing the lunches. I learned to do it all, from the lowliest job to the highest, and I worked hard ... until 1975.

That year another kind of tragedy struck, and the world I had built with years of hard work again came crashing down. I was diagnosed as suffering from emphysema, and my doctor said that I would not live long. I also suffered from as many as thirty-three different allergies, and the lining of my stomach had been destroyed by the powerful drugs I was forced to take to help me breathe.

A Foretaste of Glory Divine

As I will explain later, I had gotten away from church and now attended only on special occasions. All hope was now gone, and I had lost sight of every goal. Everything I had ever dreamed of in life was down the drain. I became suicidal, not wanting to live any longer, not seeing anything to live for. I was a wreck looking for a place to happen.

Thank God, He intervened! It was while I was in this deplorable condition that I met Jesus in a new and wonderful way.

The Greatest Sermon I Ever Heard

THE GREATEST SERMON I EVER heard in my life was delivered in that restaurant one day, and it consisted of just four words: "There's hope in Jesus." Buddy Makepeace, a man who weighed three hundred and fifty pounds, said this to me one day as he was leaving the restaurant, and then he invited me to attend a Full Gospel Businessmen's meeting. Strangely, I went.

I didn't really want to go, and if I had not promised him that I would, I almost surely would not have gone. But I had always been taught that if you promise somebody something, you should keep your word. That's the only reason I went. But that was the night I met Jesus in that new and marvelous way.

I didn't have anything left to offer Him. I hardly had a life. My body was deteriorating, and I was despondent, but that night Jesus did something so very wonderful for me.

The person who was speaking that night sang a song, "Rise and Be Healed in the Name of Jesus." I hadn't planned to respond, but I felt someone pulling my hands upward. I turned around to tell whoever was doing it to stop, but there was nobody behind me. Then, I couldn't get my hands back down.

I felt a trembling beginning in my knees, and my legs began to do something I hadn't planned on and didn't have a desire to do. I stood up.

There I was standing with my hands up in the air, tears streaming down my face, my legs unable to bend so that I could sit back down, and my hands wouldn't come back down either. It was like being in a trance, but I was unable to do anything except weep.

Peggy Makepeace, the wife of the brother who had told me there was hope in Jesus, came to me and asked if I would like to rededicate my life to Jesus. I attended church all through childhood and was there every time the church door was open. But in more recent years, because of my work, I had gotten away from it.

It started one day when I decided to leave church ten minutes early to get to work. Then the ten minutes turned into fifteen, and then thirty, and then forty ... until it seemed useless to even go to church. That had been a terrible mistake I now realized, but I had met Jesus again and in this very wonderful way.

I was totally changed that night and began praying and seeking God's face regularly, reading the Bible every day and loving on Him. From that very first night, all fear of dying went out of my life, and I had no more thoughts of suicide. I knew I would live, and I had something to live for.

I was no longer filled with sadness, disappointment, and discouragement. Jesus had taken that all away in a moment's time, and in its place, had given me that joy which is unspeakable and full of glory. I had never known joy like this before, but now it came, and it has never left me since.

Twenty-one days later I met Jesus again, and this time I saw Him. I didn't see Him as a person, but as a great light. It happened at three o'clock in the morning, and for the next three days, I sang a song God had given to me. I heard Jesus singing it inside of me, so I sang it on the outside. The song said, "By My Stripes, You are Healed." As the Lord declared that I was healed, I believed Him and threw my medications away.

A Foretaste of Glory Divine

Instead of getting better, however, I got worse. I awakened in the night gasping for every breath and unable to get relief. Everyone who knew encouraged me to go back to the doctor, to go to the drugstore and get a new prescription. I had been buying the same medications from that druggist for years, so I could just tell him that I had lost my medicine bottle and ask for a new one. But something happened on the inside of me, and I heard myself saying, "If I live, I live, and if I die, I die. If I live, I'm going to live for Jesus, and if I die, I'm going to die for Jesus. But I am not going to take any more of that medicine." And I didn't.

Soon I was gasping for every breath, and it looked like I would not survive for long, but still that song kept going through me. Jesus was still singing. He had a special song for me, and He sang it and kept on singing it. I sometimes still hear Him singing that song today, these many years later.

About three o'clock one morning, I experienced the worst attack yet. I couldn't breathe and was coughing with every attempt. At the same time, every single part of my body ached, even my bones. I literally had to crawl across the floor to get to the bathroom. Then, suddenly, as I was in that terribly weakened condition, a beautiful bright and illuminating light filled my room, and I could feel it spreading its warmth down on me. It actually felt like a garment being placed over me, and when that light touched me, the coughing stopped, and all the pain went out of my body. At the same time, there was a peace, a rest, and a calmness that came to me. It all happened in a moment's time, just that quickly.

I was left astonished, just sitting there on the floor, bathed in that light, and not yet realizing that Jesus had given me two brand new lungs and a brand new lining in my stomach.

At the same time, I was delivered from all those different allergies. Surely this was the same light that had touched Paul on the road to Damascus!

I had met Jesus twenty-one days before as my Savior, and now I had met Him as my Great Physician, and He has been my physician ever since. I haven't had to take any more medications, for He is my medicine. He is also my vitamins. He has kept me all these years.

Like my mother before me, I could now sing in the face of tragedy and that song of rejoicing brought me great victories.

Brought Back from Those Very Black Waters

ANOTHER TIME, SOME YEARS LATER, I again desperately needed God's healing power. I had gone to Nepal to trek through the Himalayan Mountains, taking the Gospel to many previously unreached villages, and I got dysentery so bad that I eventually became unconscious. The people I was with wondered if I would make it, but in that unconscious state, I saw God's light again. I could faintly hear a sister praying over me, although it seemed to me as if she were a million miles away.

In my unconsciousness, I saw a tiny ship upon some very black waters. The little ship bobbed up and down, and as the waves came, they washed over it, pushing it down into the deeper water. As I watched this, I saw appear on the bottom of that tiny ship a pinprick of light, no bigger than the head of a needle, but that light had the power to push the ship back up through those dark waters and bring it back to the surface.

I watched it do this time and time again, and then I saw a little passage and somehow knew that if that little ship could go through such a tiny passage, then I would be all right. I had the understanding that I was that little ship, and I saw that little pinpoint of light begin to guide me right through to a place of safety. As I passed through the narrow gap, consciousness came back, and God delivered me and set me free from that terrible sickness.

This has been my life, one miracle after another: the miracle of a girl from a poor farm family traveling the nations, bringing the message of Christ to men and women everywhere, the miracle of such a hopeless person becoming the leader of a worldwide ministry. It all began with a mother who refused to accept defeat, a woman who sang of blessed assurance when, it seemed, there was none. Mom's faith for *A Foretaste of Glory Divine* infected my life too.

Part II

Stories from My Childhood

Those Wooden Pegs

WHILE WE WERE GROWING UP in North Carolina, the little old house we lived in way out in the country was put together with wooden pegs, not nails. If you would crawl under it, you could see where the beams were connected with those hand-carved pegs. Under our modern houses in the South, we have small crawl spaces, but that house sat very high off of the ground, and, as children, we played under there.

The house was not insulated at all, and there was no paint on it — either inside or out. It had a simple tin roof on it, so that when it rained it made a wonderful sound. I still love that sound to this day.

When we first moved to that house, I was just three years old. There was a very small kitchen, but that kitchen had a fireplace and a stove over in the corner. It also had a cupboard. Later, a larger kitchen was added, and that became the biggest room in the house. We needed the extra space, for our family had grown to seven children: J.C., myself, William, Jerry, James, Louise, and David. Now we could all nine sit around the kitchen table together.

But in that little house, with no paint on its walls and no curtains at its windows, there was great joy. While we didn't have a lot, as far as money was concerned, we were doing all right, and everything seemed wonderful.

I remember having a fire in that fireplace in the kitchen. We hung an old black pot over the fire from a chain that hung down for that purpose, and we could hear that pot sizzling. It might have beans in it, or collards, or some other wonderful dish.

Sometimes, at night, we used an old popcorn popper with a long handle on it and a little place where you poured the popcorn into it, and we would hold that over the open fire until the kernels popped. If I close my eyes, I can go back to that little room and smell the fresh-popped corn.

On the wood heater or sitting in another pot, in winter there would occasionally be some hot lemonade that we were allowed to drink before we went to bed. What a treat that was!

We had no down comforters or electric blankets to keep us warm, so we would gather around the fire and get as warm as possible and then run and jump into a cold bed.

That was way before television became commonplace, but at the time we didn't even have a radio. We lived a very isolated or sheltered existence.

During those early years, I never knew this thing called poverty. You don't know poverty until you are taught poverty. In one sense, we didn't have a whole lot, but in another sense, we had a whole lot. We didn't have money, but we had food, and we had shelter over our heads. Ours wasn't a beautiful house like we might see somewhere down the road, but in it we had a good time, and it left us a lot of wonderful memories.

Even though our family didn't have the habit of getting together to pray as a family or read the Bible as a family, we were all required to go to church every time the church door was open. There was no such thing as saying, "I am not going today." You'd better not even look like you didn't want to go, because you were going, whether you liked it or not. We were a Christian family and were taught many sound Christian principles.

When I started school, I saw something I had never seen before. I saw girls with pretty dresses on, I saw girls with pretty bows in their hair, and I saw girls with crinoline slips. When they walked, you could hear them rustling. I surely had never seen anything like that before.

Lady Jane Lowder

I also learned that there were people who had running water in their houses, and they even had inside toilets. My thought was that it must smell pretty bad to have a toilet right there inside your house.

I also now began to see myself in a new light, as a person in need. I never knew what it was to have a need before. I had never known that I was any different from anyone else, that we lived any different than anyone else, or that there were such wonderful things out there to be had.

I never had a hot dog until I was nine or ten, and I had never felt deprived for a minute. Now suddenly I did. I say this for a reason: all too often we begin to get a concept of who we are by looking around at others. When we see somebody else having something we don't have or doing something we've never been able to do, we begin to want the things they have and to want to live the way they live.

As a result of this, other thoughts now came to us. Why *didn't* we have the things others had? Why *didn't* we do what others did? The logical answer seemed to be that our parents were not doing something they should have been doing, something other parents *were* doing, and we resented it.

All sorts of thoughts come to children's minds: Why is their house painted and ours is not? Why do they have green grass in their yard, and we sweep our dirt? Why do they mow, and we don't? Instead, we went out and got some brush, tied it together to fashion a crude broom, and swept the yard with it.

When I was just nine or ten, Dad had his stroke, and things suddenly got much worse for us. The owner of the house let us continue to live there without paying any rent, which, looking back on it, was a wonderful miracle from the Lord. But still life was hard for us.

Then, just two years later, the barn burned. What a sight that was to see ... your own barn burning. We never knew for sure what caused that fire. Some thought it was the wet hay that set itself on fire, but others thought the fire might have been set on purpose. Why someone would do that, I'm not sure.

Anyway, as soon as we saw the fire, J.C. and I ran down there to see if we could get the animals out. Cows don't have a natural fear of fire, so they won't run from it. We had to pick the calves up and throw them out the back, hoping that the fall would not kill them.

Eventually Dad shouted to us to get out because the roof was about to cave in. He was right, and so J.C. picked me up and threw me out too, before escaping himself. I hit the ground hard, but I was okay.

Lady Jane Lowder

Our family was not okay. The cows were sold and we lost that income. After this blow, nothing was left to the family but to go on Welfare, and that brought a terrible stigma on us, much like being sent to the Poor House in early Colonial days. Now, we were not just poor; we were on Welfare.

As I matured, I was obsessed with the thought of escaping this terrible fate. I would work as hard as I could work, and I would do whatever I was asked to do. I simply had to escape from that shameful place known as Welfare.

When I got to high school, I chose not to eat in the school cafeteria because I didn't want to receive the free lunches anymore. I could have received them, but I refused.

When I found the dish-washing job, I was delighted. I made those dishes sparkle. I made those pots and pans look like new.

Dad had accompanied me to work that first day. He sat there with me in the booth and gave me some very sound advice that has helped me immensely through the years.

"Sis," he said, "this is what you do: First, you come to work ten minutes early, and be ready to go to work before it's time for your shift to begin. Then, when it comes time for you to get off at night, work a little bit over. Make sure that everything is finished and you've done everything you're supposed to do, whatever the clock says. Give your boss another ten minutes or so. If you're going to be a dishwasher, then be a good one, and do your job right."

I worked hard and I did what Dad told me to do. I always arrived at work a little early, and I always quit a little late. I stayed until I was sure everything that needed to be done was done.

In other words, I made myself available to those over me, put my heart into the job, and gave a fair day's work for the fair day's pay. In the process, I became a good dishwasher and pot washer, and that meant I didn't stay long in the pot room. Before long, my boss was asking me to do other things. Once I had mastered that job, little by little, I began to see that there was a way out. If I could gradually master each job in the restaurant, I could keep moving up in position and salary.

It didn't happen overnight, but I had a determination, a mind set on coming out from Welfare, and in time, every member of my family escaped its cruel clutches.

Calamity Jane

MY GROWING-UP YEARS WERE NOT idyllic, and I was not an angel in any sense of the word. In fact, when I was a young girl, my brothers got in the habit of calling me Calamity Jane because everywhere I went, it seems, I brought trouble. They would say, "Look out! Here comes Old Calamity." I didn't really know what they meant at the time, but now that I understand it, I don't think it was very nice of them. But I guess they had a point. I had a lot to learn in life. Imagine Calamity Jane one day becoming Lady Jane! Isn't God good?

Getting My Mouth Washed Out with Soap

WHEN OUR PARENTS HEARD US use bad language of any kind, they either washed our mouths out with soap or did something worse. I know what it is to have my mouth washed out with lye soap.

We made our own soap on the farm, so I knew what went into that soap, and when I got it used on my mouth, I would run out the door, feeling sick. I was careful to shut the door behind me in a nice way, but when I got outside and out of earshot of my parents, all that was in my heart came rushing out of my mouth into the empty air (or the ears of whoever might be listening nearby). What is in the heart has a way of coming out.

One morning, when we were still quite young, my brother, J.C., was down at the barn, and he noticed that somehow the fence wire had come apart, and some of the pigs had gotten out. He came and got me, and we went back down there to mend the fence.

We had a little device that helped us stretch the wire so that we could staple it. I did the stretching, and J.C. did the stapling.

There was snow on the ground that day, and it was as cold as it could be out there. Shivering in the cold, I held the wire as tight as I could get it, and as J.C. was driving the staple in, he missed and hit his finger. Suddenly, out of his mouth came words that you would never have imagined being in there. And it just so happened that Dad was in the barn and heard it all.

He came out then and said, "J.C., it's kind of cold out here, isn't it?"

J.C. said, "Yep."

Dad said, "That kind of hurt when you hit your finger didn't it?"

J.C. said, "Yep."

Dad said, "But that doesn't give you permission to speak those things that I heard coming out of your mouth, and I'll take care of that when I get back to the house." And he did. He took care of it with a belt.

Of course, that didn't take care of the matter in J.C.'s heart. Only the blood of Jesus can change us from the inside out. J.C. doesn't mind me telling this story on him. He has plenty to tell on me.

The Wonderful Fruits of Harvest

WHEN WE WERE STILL CHILDREN ON the farm, we looked forward to Thanksgiving Day, which always came toward the end of harvest. For weeks leading up to Thanksgiving we had been experiencing those wonderful corn shucking gatherings. The wheat had already been put in the bins, the little sugar cane we raised had already been harvested, milo had already come in, oats had been put up, tomatoes had already been canned, potatoes — both the white and the sweet — had been dug, and the beans had already been canned. Everything had been prepared for that wonderful day.

There was always something very wonderful about those corn-shucking evenings when the whole community would gather together and sit talking and working together around a huge pile of corn that had been harvested. We worked in the fields all day, so these events had to be held at night. Every neighbor was present, and they were seated in families. Only the smallest children, those incapable of doing the work, were allowed to go outside and play Hide and Seek. That was great fun for them, especially when the moon was out.

A few of the women remained in the house. They had been making preparations for this community event all day long, but the work was not yet finished. They had made sweet potato pies and apple pies. They had killed chickens and cooked every type of dish, getting ready for this fellowship around the corn pile. Everyone was happy and thankful for the harvest that had come in, and this was great fun for us all.

As we sat and shucked the ears of corn one by one, the corn was then thrown into the middle (in front of us), and the shucks were thrown behind, to be dealt with later. Everyone knew that a great feast awaited, but nobody ate a bite until the last piece of corn had been shucked, sometimes starting at seven in the evening and finishing after midnight, depending on how big the pile was and how many neighbors were able to come help.

When the work was finally finished, then came the food. There was an abundance of it, and it was carried out and placed on a large table. On one end, there was a big pot of hot chicken stew, and on the other end there was a big pot of oyster stew. In between those two, were all kinds of sandwiches, all kinds of beans and corn, all kinds of pies, cakes, and other sweet things.

Sometimes there would be someone who had brought along a guitar, a fiddle, or some other musical instrument, and now, as we ate, we sang. Some of our songs were spiritual, and we gave thanks to the Lord, and some were just fun songs. It was a time of rejoicing because we had successfully brought in the harvest.

Sometimes, depending on whether there was dew on the ground or not, we children would begin putting the shucks up. If there was dew that night, we couldn't put them up. We had to wait until the sun came up the next day and dried them out. Usually it was the next day when we cribbed the corn and barned the shucks.

These were important community events as they brought us all together as a great family. We were thankful to God and to each other, and the mood was always festive. Harvest is always a reason for rejoicing.

In the days leading up to Thanksgiving, my

brothers would go out hunting. If they didn't get a turkey, then we would have chicken, but most of the time they were able to bag a wild turkey. Sometimes we had a goose, but we always had either turkey, goose, or chicken. There was never a Thanksgiving Day that we went without.

And there was always squirrel meat. People of our century find it difficult to believe that we ate those tiny creatures (and they were a lot of work), but they were delicious. All of this was in preparation for Thanksgiving, a day of thanks.

I didn't yet have an understanding of the fact that every day is a day that the Lord has made, and that we should give Him thanks every day because He has brought us to that day and helped us to enter into the gate of salvation, into His courts, to lift up our voices, and to give Him praise and thanksgiving for all the good things He has done. At least we had one day for thanksgiving.

I remember Thanksgiving the year my dad had his stroke. That happened in August, and he stayed in the hospital quite a long time. When he was eventually released, he was unable to speak, unable to walk, and couldn't raise his hands. At that moment, our life ahead looked very bleak. How could we run a farm without Dad's help? Still, we had a wonderful Thanksgiving that year.

A Foretaste of Glory Divine

The years to come were difficult, and we went steadily downhill in respect to what we could have and not have, but we had learned that it was not what we had in our hands that counted, but what we had in our hearts. God had given us His salvation and caused the earth to bring forth abundantly for us, and we were confident that He would not fail us in the years ahead.

If nothing else, growing up in rural North Carolina was an adventure, but I realize now that many of the things I learned on the farm, the early rising, the hard work, and the teamwork were all preparation for what God had in store for me in the future. He was giving me *A Foretaste of Glory Divine*.

Part III

Stories about Being Newly Saved

Walking in Darkness

FOR MANY YEARS I WALKED IN darkness, but during that time, God sent various people into the restaurant to share His Word with me. Sometimes it was over lunch, and sometimes it was just after a person had finished eating. Sometimes, as I was waiting on their table, they would talk to me about the love of God. I always had in the back of my mind the same pat answer for each one of them: "You've got your religion, and I've got mine. You keep yours, and I'll keep mine." I never said it, but I surely was thinking it.

Because I worked in the public and served so many individuals, I probably had more people tell me about Jesus than the average person does. On Sundays, groups came into the restaurant from all the various churches in the area. There were Methodists, Baptists, Presbyterians, Lutherans, Church of God, Assembly of God, and every other kind of church. These were our customers, and all of them had something to say about their faith. So I heard the Gospel of Jesus often and had many little red books and many little tracts placed in my hand.

I never threw any of them away, never tore them up, and never allowed any of my staff members to tear them up either. If they didn't want them, they could bring them to me. I respected the Word of God, even though I wasn't walking in it, and even though I wasn't living the Word of God and didn't want the Word of God to come too close to me. The reason, of course, was that my eyes were blinded to the Gospel. Thank God, He didn't give up on me and knew how to reach me when my hour of desperation came and I was ready to obey Him.

The Odd Reaction of Other Religious People to My Changed Life

NOT LONG AFTER I HAD GOTTEN SAVED and God had healed my lungs, a Presbyterian pastor came into the restaurant, and I was telling him about these miracles. He said to me, "The next thing you will be telling me is that you believe that the little boy actually brought his fish and bread to Jesus, and He fed a multitude with it."

I hadn't expected a comment like that to come from a pastor, because I thought everybody who was a Christian believed the Bible. He then went into great detail to tell me what he believed really happened that day. He said the little boy had given his food and, because a child had made such a sacrifice, this caused everybody else who was there to give what they had brought. Because it was like a family reunion, they all broke bread and had plenty left over.

Lady Jane Lowder

Even though I was still a very young Christian, I said to him, "That's your imagination. I imagine it a very different way. I believe the little boy brought the fish and bread, just like the Bible says he did. Jesus blessed it, and, with it, He fed that multitude."

He said, "Well, now I guess you're going to tell me that you believe Jonah was in the belly of that fish?"

I said, "Yes, sir, I am telling you that. I believe that Jonah took a ride in that whale."

He said, "Now, Jane, come on! Let common sense take hold of your brain."

I said, "I believe that the fish did swallow him, and I believe he *was* in the belly of that whale for three days. I believe that the fish heard God's voice, I believe he threw Jonah up, and I believe Jonah then went running to do what God had told him to do."

I didn't know if I was being arrogant or not, but I was taking up for what I believed. It shook me to think there were pastors who didn't believe in the Bible.

That was just the beginning of my shock. A few weeks later I received the Holy Ghost, and suddenly my Methodist pastor no longer wanted to talk to me, the associate pastor didn't want to talk to me, and the Baptist pastor who had come to see me every time I was in the hospital didn't want to talk to me. I thought, "All these people loved me ... until I got the Holy Ghost. And now they don't even want to talk to me."

I went to my pastor, and he said, "I will talk to you, but not today, another day" (which day has never yet come). I went to the associate pastor and caught him just as he was going through a buffet line in a restaurant. I asked him if I could come and talk to him about the baptism of the Holy Spirit and speaking in other tongues. He said, "Not tonight. Maybe tomorrow or some other time." That "other time" has never come.

That Baptist pastor and his wife, bless their hearts, had been very good to me for years. I had been in the hospital often, and they had always come with their Bibles and had prayed and spoken the Word of God over my life. But, now, after I had received the baptism of the Holy Spirit, they wanted nothing more to do with me. That broke my heart because I loved them, and I really believed that they loved me. For some reason, they just couldn't deal with the Holy Ghost.

He told me, "We don't believe in swinging from the chandeliers."

I thought, "My Lord, where does that come from?"

I said to him, "We don't have chandeliers in the church I attend (I had started going to an Assembly of God church). Do you have chandeliers in yours?" I didn't have a clue what he was talking about. Later, I understood what he was trying to say, but at the moment I was totally confused, trying to envision people swinging from the chandeliers in some church.

Those were my experiences in the first two months of my Christian life, after I had been totally renewed and healed by the Lord. I quickly learned that not all those who called themselves Christians were willing to obey God completely or take Him at His Word.

Having a Testimony to God's Glory

NOT TOO LONG AFTER I CAME to know the Lord, I was visiting a church with my sister way up in the mountains. It was a different kind of church, not like our usual Methodist or Baptist church. This one was Pentecostal, and they believed that the Spirit of God would move sovereignly upon someone in the congregation, and they would have the message for the day. I have since noticed that there are other churches that have this practice.

I went back to that church on Sunday, and they had a time of giving testimonies. A woman stood and talked for twenty minutes or so about how bad her husband was, the bad things that had happened in her home, things he had said, things he had done, things here and there and everywhere, and then she had the audacity to ask the people of the church to pray that he would get saved and come to the church. Could anyone have imagined that man would have a half a chance if he got saved and came to that church? Everybody there would say to him, "You beat your wife, you were a drunkard, you did this, you did that?" That woman had just opened her life to everyone in the community and made her home the subject of gossip for everyone to enjoy. I was a new Christian, and I thought, "Lord, what is all this about?"

Others stood and gave their testimonies, many speaking the same type of things. God spoke to me and said, "I want you to give a testimony, but I want you to give a testimony about the power of My blood to cleanse and set free and give new life." When the others had finished, I stood up and gave my testimony. It didn't take long because I was just starting out. Amazingly everybody started clapping when I finished. I had been terribly nervous about doing it, but now I was blessed because I had done what the Lord had told me to do, and others had been blessed by it.

When we testify, we don't have to tell everything about what is going on in our lives or about people who might be hurting us in some way. Instead, we are glorify God, and lift Him up, and He will draw others to Himself. I was enjoying more of *A Foretaste of Glory Divine*.

Part IV

Early Stories from Camp

My First Days at Camp

THE FIRST DAY I WAS HERE ON THE campground in Ashland, Virginia, I had come because God Himself told me to and because Brother Lloyd Ashby and his wife, who were then pastoring in our hometown (Sanford, North Carolina), brought me and another sister.

I worked all day that day on the office building that was then under construction. I scraped and painted walls and, in the process, learned that God had delivered me from my allergy to paint. It no longer bothered me.

Many potentially negative things happened to me that day. For instance, on my way to the restroom, I was bitten by a dog that lived here at the time. And that was just for starters. Many other interesting things happened that day. But the good far outweighed the bad.

That evening, as we were eating dinner in the camp dining hall, a sister who had lived here for many years, served as the camp treasurer, and traveled to many nations for God, asked me if I would like to go to her house and take a shower before we left to go back home. She was one of the very few who had their own house. Most of the camp people lived in common housing areas.

I had heard that some unusual things were happening in this sister's house, particularly that many were receiving words of prophecy, being slain in the Spirit, and spending much time in prayer. Consequently, I said to the Lord, before I went across the campground to her house, "I don't want to be slain in the Spirit, because I want to hear every word that is spoken in her house. I don't want to miss a thing."

While we were still eating, some of those who lived on the campground brought me some clothes they called "preaching clothes." I took a look at those clothes and said to myself, "I am *not* wearing these clothes." But I accepted them anyway. I didn't want to be ugly to anyone, and whatever the Lord gives us we should receive with thanksgiving in our hearts. Before it was over, there was a whole box of those clothes, and I took them all and put them in Pastor Ashby's car to take them home with me. My idea was that when I got home I would pack them up and mail them back to the camp.

A Foretaste of Glory Divine

Now, as I went over to the sisters house, I was still insisting in my spirit that I did not want to be slain in the Spirit, because I wanted to hear everything that went on. As I went through the front door, I saw that my other lady companion from Sanford had just come out of the bathroom. She had finished her shower and had gotten dressed. As she came into the living room, the lady of the house stretched her hand toward her, and I saw her falling. I said to the Lord again, "I do not want to be slain in the Spirit." Then, suddenly, the lady wheeled around, pulled a dress out of her closet, and said, "You can put this on after you take your shower." I hadn't brought any extra clothes with me, other than the ones I was wearing, so I took it. As she handed me the dress, she said, "This is your first preaching dress."

I thought to myself, "Well, I have a whole bunch of what they are calling 'preaching dresses' out there in the car, and I don't have any intention of putting any of them on."

After I had taken my shower, I did put that dress on, and then I came back out. Just as I was coming down the hall and into the living room, out came that hand again, and five hours later I got up from the floor. I hadn't heard a word that went on around me during those five hours, but during all that time

God had been showing me wonderful things. I now knew that I was going to go home, quit my job, and come back and live at this place (although I thought it would just be for a season), and I also knew that I was going to go around the world and preach the Gospel of Jesus Christ.

Over the years, Calvary Campground had developed into something more than a place to gather and hear good preaching every summer. Because the founding family, the Heflins, all had a burden for the nations and traveled and ministered often in farflung places, men and women who shared that vision had begun to make the camp their home. They would help out with the campmeetings (winter and summer) and the many conferences, they would train under the able leadership of the camp, and then they would go out after campmeeting was over and minister wherever they found people hungry for God. I now felt led to join them.

There was a lot more that God showed me in those hours. For instance, I saw visions of myself dancing in the Spirit, and I had never done anything like that before. We just didn't do these things in the Methodist church.

In my vision, my hands were lifted up toward Heaven, and my feet were dancing. Once I had gotten up from the floor that evening, I understood that this was exactly what I had been doing down there. I was moving my feet in every direction, speaking in tongues, laughing and crying, and many other things.

During my time on the floor that night, after showing me many other things, one of the last things the Father showed me was Jesus coming. He was standing riding on a cloud. That night God made Jesus' coming so absolutely, fantastically, and marvelously real to me that every part of my body was crying out for His coming. It couldn't have been more real.

I hadn't really known the Scriptures about the cloud He went up on and the cloud He will come back on. God taught me all that in visions.

We finally left this place at about twelve thirty that night, and it took us four or five hours to get home. In the car, as we were on our way, God again showed me that vision of Jesus' coming, and I can still see it and feel the urgency of it today.

These experiences were all wonderful, so wonderful that I now walked around looking up because I was convinced that Jesus could come that very day. I'm convinced that it is God's will for each of us to have this kind of expectancy, that today is the day He could very well come.

Lady Jane Lowder

In those days, people would sometimes ask me, "What are you looking for?" "Why are you looking up in the sky?" Because I was looking up so expectantly, others who walked by me sometimes looked up too and asked, "What are you looking at?" That gave me the opportunity to tell them what I was looking for.

I couldn't wait until I got to work that next day to tell my boss that I was resigning. I called him at his home at seven o'clock that morning (something you just did not do) and told him what was happening.

Nobody who knew me could believe what I was doing. I had worked in that particular restaurant faithfully for the past sixteen years and had a total of twenty-two years in restaurant work. I liked my job, I liked what I was doing, I liked working with people, and I liked working with food. "You won't quit," everyone told me, but God severed me from that place and from that job. During the last twenty-one days I worked, I fasted, preparing myself for what was to come, and from there, I never looked back and never had a desire to go back. God had called me to something higher.

There were several of us who came to camp about the same time from North Carolina. There was the sister who had accompanied me that first day, and the man who had led me to Christ and his wife. We didn't know for sure how long we would be here, and some had a longer season than others. The single sister, for instance, went on to work in Israel, got married while serving there, and is now living in Japan. After being here for a few years, the couple went back to Sanford and did evangelism and traveled some for the Lord in other countries. The gentleman has since gone on to be with the Lord. After thirty-seven years, I am still here.

We arrived here on a Thursday, and you would have thought that since everyone in leadership knew we were coming, they would have prepared a place for us to stay. But it was not so. I was assigned a room in what was called the Green Doors Building, the first room on the back side, but that room turned out to be packed full of "stuff," and there was mildew halfway up the wall. We first had to empty the room. Then we had to wash down the walls. We would need to get some beds set up in there before the end of the day, if we were to stay there. The wife of the pastor who had first brought us sat outside watching us and weeping. She could not believe that we could move into that room.

Another girl who had come to the camp at about the same time was assigned as my roommate.

Lady Jane Lowder

Together we washed down those walls with Chlorox water, took all the stored furniture out, put our little bags in that room, and went to bed as happy as a couple of larks.

My first assignment at camp was to the dish washing room, and that would remain my assignment for the next twenty-some years. Other things were added to that assignment, but the responsibility over the dish room was never removed. Two other huge assignments that were added were my duties for the kitchen (picking up food from the food bank and other suppliers) and dining hall (overseeing the cleaning of the floors), and the snack bar. The responsibility over the snack bar ended only in 1998.

Each year, during camptime, I was head over the snack bar. Mother Heflin told me that this was where God had told her to put me, and so that is where I went.

I accepted my assignment, but I did have a question for God: Why had He just delivered me so miraculously from restaurant work, and now He was putting me back into that same atmosphere? After I got prayed through on the subject, I loved the work.

On my first night in the kitchen, I was carrying a stack of heavy Syracuse china dishes when I suddenly realized that there was a place in God, a special anointing that literally took the weight out of things. This was the same plateware that was being used in most restaurants. It was heavy because it was built for heavy use, so that it would not break easily. When you had a stack of ten or more of those dishes in your hands, they were quite heavy. I was bringing them out of the dish room and putting them out on shelves in the dining room, when suddenly I realized that they had no weight to them at all. It felt like I was carrying feathers.

At first I thought my brain must have gone crazy, but when I got another stack and set off with them, I found that they, too, were weightless.

I knew that china well. It was the same china we had been using in the restaurant, and I marveled over the fact that those plates were now weightless.

I didn't know anything yet about the anointing. In fact, I hardly knew that there was such a thing or that God could anoint you to do certain tasks. And yet the china was weightless, and I continued to marvel over that fact long after we had finished putting everything away.

There was a lady here who was working in the kitchen at the time, and she came out and stood near me and said, "I would like to pray for you." I remember her saying to me, "The book of Ezekiel is going to hold great meaning for your life, and God will open this book up to you." I didn't know anything about Ezekiel at the time, but as she prayed for me, I was caught away in the Spirit for about an hour. During that time, God again showed me the vision of Jesus coming down on the cloud. This time it was accompanied by the ringing of the camp bell, and I suddenly found myself wanting to run to every nearby house, knock on the door, and tell anyone who would listen that Jesus was coming.

Those were my experiences for the first three years of my life on this campground — the most wonderful years of my life. Nothing was difficult! Nothing! It was all so very wonderful.

This was not true in the natural, of course. For instance, the sewer was not so wonderful in those days, and there was often a smell of sewage around the camp, but I didn't let that bother me. Nothing bothered me. Nothing! I was somewhere up in the clouds.

We had three services every day, four counting the Young People's Service, we served three complete meals, and then we washed all the dishes and put them back in their place, getting out of the dining hall after each meal just in time to get to the next service. And everyone was required to be in all the services. Once I got down to the tabernacle and got into the presence of God, I was re-charged and ready to go again. Being in every service was not a burden for me. I loved it.

The famous and powerful R.W. Schambach was ministering here at the camp that first weekend, and so the place was packed. People were hanging out of the windows, and our work load was especially great. I didn't mind.

After the last service of the day, I went to the snack bar and worked there until one or one thirty in the morning. Then I went to the treasurer's house and helped her count the change that had come in the offering, and I would get back to my room about three or three thirty in the morning.

Those nights were very short, so we had to pray for the Lord to multiply our sleep. I would get up again by five thirty or six in the morning to be in the dish room on time. And it was all absolutely wonderful! Absolutely wonderful!

Why can I say this? Because after all of this, then we were able to see the lives of the people who had come changed, and just as their lives were being changed, mine was being changed too. There was nothing beautiful about Calvary Campground, but there was something very wonderful about it, something incredibly wonderful.

The walls of the dining room were whitewashed, since that was the cheapest thing available, and the bare concrete floors were painted gray. I can't tell you how many times I swabbed those floors. That was part of my responsibility, so if no one else did it, I had to.

No one was allowed to remain behind in the dining hall cleaning during service times. So the only time we had to clean that room was after eleven at night (sometimes long after).

When a young family from New York came to live at camp for that second summer, they took the cleaning of the dining hall on as their own personal responsibility and faithfully did it every night. Thank God for them.

Many people stayed on after camptime was over, and so even in wintertime, we had four people living in every available room, using bunk beds. If you left the camp to go overseas preaching, you were required to move everything out of your room and store it. It all had to be packed up, and then, when you came back, you usually were assigned a different room.

In summertime, when many visitors were coming for the summer activities, all of us who lived in Green Doors had to vacate our rooms during the ten weeks of Summer Camp and were put somewhere else, so that the visitors would have a place to stay.

During my first year of campmeeting, Mother Heflin assigned me a small cabin, the first one next to the tabernacle. She told me about it the day before camp opened. It was full of stored items that would have to be moved. At the same time, she told me she wanted me to clean the snack bar and get it ready for the summer.

The existing snack bar was very primitive. It had a dirt floor and was surrounded by nothing but chicken wire. When I went in to examine it, I found that the tables were covered with a deep dust, plus they were piled high with items that there was no other place to store at the moment. She told me to choose which was more important, my room or the snack bar. I chose the snack bar. Another lady and I got a part of the single gallon of Chlorox that was to be shared among everybody on the campground. Camp didn't have much money at the time, but we did have a big God.

After we had cleared out and cleaned the snack bar, I went to examine the place she had told me I could live in and found that it was literally piled to the ceiling with "stuff." Four windowpanes were missing, and I couldn't close the door because it was off of the hinges. I thought to myself, "There is no time to do this." I put all my clothes back in the car and said to myself, "I'll find a place to stay tomorrow." So campmeeting had started, and I didn't have a place to sleep.

After I got out of the snack bar that first night, I went to see what was called Building #1. The upstairs was not yet finished inside; it was just two by four studs with no sheetrock on them, and yet many of the girls were sleeping up there. I searched around and found a mattress that was not being used. I found a double sheet I had brought from home, folded it double, and crawled in between the two layers, and that's where I slept. All of my clothes were still in the car.

I was given a dress and told that I should wear it when I was on the platform. All of the camp staff were dressing alike for the services. Someone had worn this particular dress for several years already, and now I inherited it.

But I wore a size eight, and the dress they gave me was a ten, so it hung on me like a sack of potatoes. It was too big across the shoulders, and too big everywhere else. It took great grace for me to wear that dress, but I did it. I can still remember what that dress looked like, but none of those things mattered to me at the time. The great joy of

A Foretaste of Glory Divine

my life was that I was here, that Jesus had told me to come, that I was going to meet Him here, that He was going to change me, and that He would do wonderful things in and through me.

I loved every minute of it, and I made it to every service. I went to every morning service, to every afternoon service, and to every night service. I even made it to part of the Young People's Service nearly every night. I missed only part of one afternoon service when I was pulled out to paint the floor in a ladies bathroom. Other than that, I was in every service.

I was never late for dish-washing, I was never late for anything else. And I had a grand time!

Basically we had nothing, so we had to pray for everything. We had to pray for the food to come in; we had to pray for money to pay the light bill. We all felt the shared responsibility of seeing these and other needs met.

We had to push the camp bus to get it started when it was time to get everyone together to go into Richmond for the services in the church there. Every time we stopped, the old bus stalled, so we had to get out and push it again. Still, we got to church, and we got there on time. If, on the way back, someone among us wanted to stop to buy some potato chips or other snack foods, the rule was that if we couldn't buy enough for everyone or were not willing to share what we could buy, then we didn't buy any at all. These were principles that Sister Edith Heflin taught us in the early years.

I Released My Car

EARLY IN MY CAMP EXPERIENCE, GOD began to speak to me that He was going to bless me in many ways. He would give me a house here in our country and houses in other lands as well, He would provide airline tickets for me, and not only for me, but He would put finances in my hand so that I could help others meet their destinies in places around the world. The amazing thing is that these things were spoken to me way back in the 1970s, when it didn't seem that I could go anywhere or do anything at all.

One night in campmeeting I was led to release my car and pledge some finances that I didn't yet have in hand to help someone else go to Israel. No sooner had I handed the keys to my car over than a young lady who had lived in Israel for some years stood up and began to prophesy over me. She said that I would go to the nations, that God would give me finances, not only to pay a portion of the costs, but all of them, and that the time would come when people from other nations would call me to come and bless their churches and would send me the necessary tickets. At the time, I had never yet preached a single sermon (I had only given testimonies), but through the years I have seen all of that prophecy come to pass, I have come and gone and been able to bless others to go. And, yes, tickets have come from other nations, along with the invitation to come and bless their people.

One of the things God kept saying to me in those days was that He wanted to give me a new wardrobe, new shoes, and everything else that went with it. And God has done that too. He has poured out abundantly upon my life. In one short span alone, He blessed me with ten new skirts and five new outfits and there have been countless coats, shoes, watches, bags, perfume, and finances. How good God is!

"They're Coming!"

THAT FIRST YEAR AT CAMP, everything was new for me. Each day, after our morning prayer time, Brother Heflin would take the microphone and say a few things to us about the importance of the work of the day. He would inevitably close by saying, "They're coming! They're coming!"

I thought to myself, "Who's coming?" Who would come way out here in the country?

And we were way out in the country. Today, it doesn't seem so far out, because the city of Richmond has expanded toward us, but when I first came here there was just one A&P Supermarket (no shopping centers like there are in Ashland today), one or two restaurants, and one or two service stations. That was it.

The camp was located on a narrow country road, and the road into the camp itself had holes in it almost as big as a truck. When it rained, it was terrible getting in and out of this place.

Lady Jane Lowder

When Brother Heflin made that statement, the dining room was packed to the ceiling with "stuff" that had been stored there the previous winter, and one of the jobs assigned to me was to clean it out. What a job that was! And that was just one of the buildings that had to be cleaned out and prepared before summer campmeeting could get started.

The tabernacle was another of the buildings that needed a lot of work. Until then, the floor of it had been just dirt and small gravel, and now someone had an idea about improving it. Many pieces of carpet had been donated to the camp by hotels and motels that were remodeling. Could these somehow be used to cover the dirt floors?

We were told that people loved to tarry around the camp altars, kneeling and even lying in God's presence for hours. When anyone was slain in the Spirit at Calvary Campground, they didn't just get right back up. They stayed in the presence of God to see what He would say to them. And that dirt floor didn't make seeking God in this way very comfortable.

The problem with the carpet pieces was that they were all different sizes, all different colors, and all cut differently. It seemed impossible to do the job with that. But that, we were told, was what God had supplied us, so we were to start cleaning it and getting it ready to cover the floor at the front of the tabernacle.

Local theaters had donated a lot of their old seating, but the seats had been disassembled and brought to the camp in pieces. They, too, were all different sizes. Now some of the men had to figure out how to piece together those seats to create adequate seating for the coming camp season.

In time, we found a way to overlap those carpet pieces and fasten them in place with nails driven into the ground around the edges. It wasn't very elegant, but it worked.

Running into a New Place

CAMP FINALLY OPENED, AND that first Saturday night the Lord spoke prophetically through me about running into His presence. I don't remember the exact words, but I was absolutely amazed when about five hundred people got up and began running around the tabernacle. I thought, "What on earth is happening?" Then it dawned on me that they were responding to what God had said. The people ran into a new place, and I began to understand in that moment that when God speaks something, if we act on it in faith something happens on the inside of us.

The next thing I knew we were running around that tabernacle believing God for nations and believing God for tickets to go to those nations.

Doing Things I Had Never Heard Of

RUNNING WAS JUST ONE OF the things we did believing for nations. We were doing things I had never heard of before. For example, we were taking maps, walking on them, lying on them, sleeping on them, dancing on them, and weeping over them. At one point, God told us to write "Jerusalem" on the bottoms of our feet and walk on them by faith.

I wrote on my hand, "Paid in Full," and then I would show that to people. They would ask what it was, and I would tell them it was my ticket around the world. Sometimes I didn't have anything at all, but I would say, "Read my hand, 'Paid in Full by Jesus Christ.'" That was our faith.

We learned that as we would stand at the altar, lifting our voices and holding up a certain country before the Lord, waving it before His face in faith, He would honor our faith to go there. We sometimes ran over to the camp prayer room and laid our hands on a map on the wall, wrote down what God was telling us, and then put it on the floor and danced on it. We did many other strange things.

Sometimes we then put that note in our shoe and walked on it until the victory came. We put certain notes under our pillows and slept on them. In this way, we walked and talked our God-given burdens every day, and God always honored us.

This may sound foolish to some, but in the end, we went to those places and preached the Gospel there. We didn't have anything but our faith, but faith is what you need to get the job done. Faith will move the hand of God on your behalf. And He has called all of us to be witnesses for Him in this needy world.

Acting in Faith

WE WERE TAUGHT TO ACT IN faith in another regard. We had no money in our pockets and hardly any food in our refrigerators, hardly enough money to get camp open for the start of campmeeting each year, but God came, He strengthened us, and a life of faith was being lived out on this campground.

When the camp freezers were empty, Sister Edith Heflin would come up and lay hands on every one of them and command food to come to them. At times, campmeeting was about to open, and Brother Wallace Heflin was declaring, "They're coming," and yet everything in the kitchen was empty. I was walking in a new place with God, and all I wanted to do was follow what He said, but our natural eyes had to look at all those empty spaces. The Heflin family had eyes to look beyond the emptiness, and they saw God's provision. Sure enough, the people came, and sure enough, God supplied for them all.

Year after year, I saw us open campmeeting with

no food in the freezers, except for a few loaves of bread and sometimes a few hundred pounds of fish that had been donated to us. God supplied as the people came.

At every mealtime, those in attendance went to the dining hall, expecting to have something good to eat, and they were never disappointed. Sister Heflin taught us to pray over empty boxes and believe God for a miracle. She taught us to pray over the food serving line, expecting the available food to multiply as it was being served up.

Those of us in the know realized that there was not enough to feed everyone, but we had been taught to ask God to multiply it and then to expect Him to do it. And He did. He provided and kept on providing, and He is still providing today, so many years later.

We learned to expect answered prayer, and God was faithful to the vision He had given to the Senior Heflins then, and He is still faithful today.

The Beginnings of Our Missionary Travels

I WAS BEGINNING TO SEE THE Lord move in many people's lives, and I was one of those people. That next year many of us were raised up to begin our travels around the nations. At first, we didn't have a clue that we would ever be able to do that, only raw faith that said, "You can because God says you can."

But we had good people standing behind us, and they told us, "You can."

"You can go, and you can make an impact on the world."

"You can go, and you can preach to thousands."

"You can go, and the giftings will flow through you."

Not only did they stand beside us and behind us, but they pushed us out there to that place of activating that word from God. And God has not changed. I want to tell you today, "You can do it too!

The Glory in the Dust

CLOUDS OF DUST ROSE UP in the tabernacle as people praised God on those old carpet strips laid out to cover the dirt floor. What a job it was to sweep those carpets every morning and get them back into place for the day!

But the glory of God would come down, and people rolled off the platform and ran around the tabernacle. Many of those who were standing straight up, looking into the face of God, would fall like cord wood in His presence.

As the years passed, little by little, we were able to improve the facilities. The dining room had been very plain, just a bare concrete block building where we could seat about five hundred people to eat. If it was damp outside, the floor would have puddles of water on it. Each year, things got better, as God miraculously supplied our needs.

Where Are Those Mops?

I USUALLY HAD VOLUNTEERS TO help me clean the dining room floor every night, but one night I went up to get started on it, and there was not a single mop anywhere to be found. I prayed, "Oh, God, show us where those mops are?"

I asked around, but nobody seemed to know where they were.

As I was looking into the face of the Lord, I said again, "Lord, where are those mops?"

He said, "Over in that cornfield."

That seemed very strange to me, but I went out, crossed over the barbed-wire fence, and soon found our mops, lying hidden in the neighboring field. At the time, I couldn't imagine who might have put them out there. As it turned out, it was some of our wonderful teenagers who didn't want to help with the mopping that night. They thought that if they could get rid of the mops, they wouldn't have to do the work, but God just showed me where those mops were, and I went and got them, and we mopped the floors anyway.

Miracle, after miracle, after miracle, happened, and they continue to happen today, because we are still believing God for our needs. He is our Source personally, and He is the Source for the ministry of the camp.

Learning the Importance of the Altar

WE WERE TAUGHT THAT WE should come to the altar to worship God. During campmeeting time, Brother Heflin and Sister Heflin both prayed over our staff people, but when it came to the church in Richmond, they taught us to leave that privilege for the visitors and seek God for ourselves.

We went to church in Richmond on Wednesday nights, Friday nights, Sunday mornings and Sunday evenings. If we had personal needs, we were to go forward and prostrate ourselves before the Lord and find Him on our own. We went forward to worship Him, but also to do business with Him.

Usually, every time we had a meeting at our church, when the altar call was given, everybody went to the altar and either lay down on their face before the Lord and talked to Him, or they stood or knelt and called out to God. The point is that it was not, for us, a time of being ministered to; it was a time when we came and ministered unto the Lord. That is where you find Him, and I believe that we need this same attitude today.

I was brought up in a church where we did not have that kind of altar call. Altar calls were only for sinners to come and get saved. Once you got saved, there was not a lot taught about coming to the altar, but the altar of God is not just for sinners. The altar of God, throughout the history of the Old Testament, was where men came to meet with God and to meet Him on His terms.

We often had people come to the camp who said they really wanted to go to the nations, but when it came time for the altar call, they were the first ones out the back door and the first ones to arrive at the snack bar to eat a hamburger and drink a coke. If they had really had a desire to go to the nations, they could have come and met God and found His will.

Anyone can find twenty minutes to spend with God, and the snack bar would have still been open for them to eat afterwards. If we make the choice to come to Him and spend time with Him, God will work in us. But we have to make that choice. Sometimes the answer doesn't come in the first five minutes you are at the altar, but if you will make the choice to linger, His presence will come, the change you seek will come, the enlightenment you need will come.

Sometimes there are visions that come with tarrying at the altar. Sister Ruth Heflin taught us that you might only see His feet at first, and you will see other things about Him only after you have tarried longer in His presence. There is nothing quite like worshipping the Lord in His holy altar!

My Grand Team

ONE DAY, AS I WAS WALKING across the campground, I felt a little discouraged about some of the things that were going on with my "team." It's wonderful to have a team, if it's working well. If it's not, it can be terrible.

My team was made up mostly of the mentally challenged. I always told them that we had the best team on camp, and if we had the best team, then we could do great things. And we did some wonderful things, things that others thought we could never do.

For instance, I would get all those young folks working together, and we could pick up very heavy objects and move them. Others marveled at this, but back home on the farm, we had been taught that if you could get many hands working together, it would diminish the heaviness of the object you wanted to move. Each of us would move only a portion of the load. So if we could get four or five or more of those seemingly-weak individuals lifting

A Foretaste of Glory Divine

together on a big log, we could get it up and load it on a truck or do whatever else had to be done with it.

But that particular day things were not going well, and I was discouraged and said to myself and to God, "I don't have to take this. I am tired of it."

I said it openly to one of the boys on my team: "I'm just not going to do this anymore. I'm leaving." I didn't mean I was leaving camp. I meant I was leaving the dish room and going for a walk.

As I walked that day, God spoke to me. He said, "If you are not yielding to discouragement, then you are overcoming, and you become an overcomer." That day I received a new understanding of what it meant to overcome. It was not the fact that I didn't feel like doing something at the moment that mattered. After I had gotten that revelation, I went back to the dish room to finish my work.

Seeing me coming back in, that young boy called out to me, "Are you going to walk out on what God has for you just because you are angry, just because you're mad? Are you just going to walk out and leave everything and not fulfill your purpose in God?" I had said similar words to them many times before, while we were all out raking leaves, and while we were doing other things together, and now he was repeating my own words back to me. That opened my eyes in a new and wonderful way. I would never give up on my destiny in God. The boy was absolutely right!

The Official Woodcutter

FOR THE FIRST FIVE YEARS I was here at camp, I was the official woodcutter, and I cut wood for the kitchen, the individual leaders' houses, and the prayer room. The next year I became the official tree feller because I knew how to operate a chain saw, how to handle an axe, and how to split wood. I had learned it all on the farm.

I particularly loved the chain saw. In fact, when I was still in grade school, I had to write a story on the subject "The Sweetest Sound to My Ears," and I wrote on the hum of the chain saw. It was then the sweetest sound to my ear, and it has remained so. I love to hear one of them in action.

This might seem very strange to some, so let me explain: To me, a chain saw sounds so much better than a crosscut saw, and, believe me, I've used them both. There is no comparison between the two in the amount of work that can be done. A chain saw takes the work out of the job.

Lady Jane Lowder

I later taught these skills to many of the camp men. I also taught some of them how to use a pick, because God had given me that ability when I was a young girl. Had I wanted to learn it back then? Probably not, but I learned it anyway because Dad said, "This is what you are going to do today," and so that was what we did. Those talents came in handy in the long run.

Unusual Miracles at Camp

CAMP HAS ALWAYS BEEN A PLACE of miracles, and we experienced them on a daily basis. For instance, one day a young man who was living here tried to open a hot radiator cap. He knew that the vehicle had overheated, but he waited until he thought it would be cool enough, and then he opened the cap. He was wrong. Hot water and steam spewed out on him, scalding his chest and his face. Those who were with him at the time took his shirt off, and his skin stuck to the shirt, coming off of his entire chest and abdomen.

Thank God that Brother Heflin was here at the time. He was fearless. He ran up and prayed for that young man. He never went to a doctor. Instead, God healed him and took away all his pain. It was a great miracle, and we grew accustomed to trusting God in every situation.

God Did It for Me, Too

I HAD MY SHARE OF THESE miracles. One day another lady and I were in the back part of the camp clearing away the underbrush. She had become my roommate at camp. She was anorexic, so I had to make sure she ate properly. She went with me everywhere I went and worked with me, and I never let her out of my sight.

That particular day I was operating the chain saw. We had felled a tree and were cutting it up, but the chain saw had run out of gas. As I was taking the cap off to put in more gas, my arm brushed the red-hot exhaust. I pulled my arm away, but my skin stayed on the hot exhaust, and my arm was seared.

My roommate just stood there looking at me, so I said, "Don't just look at me! Pray!"

"Okay," she said and then prayed, "Oh, Jesus, she's burned herself! Heal it." And God took all the pain out of it — just like that. We experienced that kind of miracle so often.

The Blood Stopped

ANOTHER DAY I WAS SPLITTING wood at Mother Heflin's house. Sometimes, when wood has a knot in it, it just doesn't split well, and sometimes it flies off in unpredictable directions. That day a piece flew up and hit me under the eye, and it began to bleed profusely. One of our young brothers was coming across the field, and I said to him, "Come and pray for me. I have hurt my face."

He came over, saw what had happened, and began to pray. He said, "Oh, God, Sister Jane is bleeding. Stop it!" And God stopped it — just like that. Those kinds of miracles were everyday for us.

My Leg Became Straight

VERY EARLY ON, I WAS IN PAIN one day as I walked across the campground. All my life I had walked with my right foot turned out, and my hip on that same side would suddenly pop out, and it would be very difficult to get back in place. When it did go back in, it was painful for a while, and if I would turn a certain way, it would pop out again. I had been down in the tabernacle, where we were putting down those carpet pieces and fastening them to the ground with nails, and my leg had begun hurting.

There was a lady living at camp who was in her late sixties or early seventies, and she was on a forty-day fast. I couldn't believe, at the time, that anybody could go on a forty-day fast. The thing I noticed about her was that every day she was singing all day long — morning, noon, and night. She was even singing as she worked, just singing away.

She had been in another place, putting down carpet, and she had smashed her finger with a hammer and knocked the nail off of it. She said, "Oh, Sister Jane, pray for my thumb." I took her thumb in my hand, and I prayed that God would heal it and take away the pain. She looked up and said, "Oh, all the pain is gone," and she went on her way singing.

I was so amazed that I just stood there with my mouth open. God had actually taken the pain out of her finger when I prayed for her. I stood on that little path and said, "God, why don't You heal my hip someday?" I didn't even ask Him to do it right then, but in that moment I felt the bone in my hip turn like a doorknob, and my leg became straight, and it has been straight ever since. That was in 1976. We were learning to walk in miracles every single day.

No Pain

WE HAD A MAN WHO WAS nearly seventy, and he was not accustomed to hard work. His wife had died, and all he had left was his little dog, so he came here to the campground to live. But nobody was ever allowed to just *be* on the campground; everybody who stayed here had to work.

This man was usually one of my workers, although not on the particular night in question. It was a special night. We had already worked all day long, but that day at suppertime, Brother Heflin had come into the dining room and said, "I don't want anybody going home tonight. We are going to work until dark backfilling the basement of the snack bar." It was summertime, and the days were very long.

We were out there backfilling the basement, and this gentleman came to me with tears in his eyes. He said, "I won't be able to get up in the morning. I'm just not used to this kind of work, and my body will be so tired I won't be able to get myself out of bed."

A Foretaste of Glory Divine

I asked him, "Are you doing this for the camp or are you doing this for Jesus?"

He said, "Well, I'm doing it for the Lord."

I said, "Then the Lord is going to give you strength, and you are not going to have any pain in your body when you get up in the morning." And I prayed for him.

That was on a Saturday night, and the next morning I saw the man coming up the path, and I went out to meet him and asked him how he felt. He said, "I feel wonderful! I don't have any pain in my body."

I said to him, "Why don't you just lift your hands and receive the Holy Ghost right now?" He did, right there in the middle of the campground.

Tempted to Leave Camp

I CAN NEVER FORGET THE DAY MY very best friends came to town to visit and then invited me out to eat. During our meal, they told me that I should get out of this place. Working every day without receiving any salary, they suggested, was just not right. I could get a good job, earn a good living, and have money to travel, if that was what I really wanted to do. As it was, my talents were being "wasted."

It all sounded very reasonable to me at the time. I could take a good job, save up some money, and then go to the nations. But I had worked long enough to know that it takes a long time to save up that kind of money, it takes a long time before you can get enough vacation time saved up, and if you don't get a paid vacation, then you can't afford to take the time off. There are always too many bills to be paid.

I had also learned that work becomes a trap for far too many. You get locked into your responsibilities and your routine until you can't go anywhere at all. Your most important responsibility is to your boss and his company, and you have made a commitment to be there during certain hours, and if you're good at what you do, they always want you to work overtime and make you feel that they can't function without you. If you don't work the desired overtime or you have to go out of town when they feel they need you, then feathers get ruffled, and the atmosphere at work becomes strained.

Thank God I didn't listen to those friends, and thank God I made the decision to be faithful to His calling on my life.

Friends are not the only ones who don't understand. Relatives who are not walking with God are also quick to tell us what we *could be* accomplishing in life and how much we *could be* making doing something else. But our goals are eternal. God's Kingdom always comes first, and we are victors when we stick with His call.

Holding On or Letting Go?

WHEN I FIRST CAME TO CAMP, there were some things I was holding on to that God had already spoken to me about letting go of. He was dealing with me in this way in order to bring about a new freedom in my life. For instance, I had some very beautiful pieces of jewelry — rings, earrings, and necklaces. Not only were they costly, but they had been given to me by people I loved.

Sometimes people give you things, and they tell you that you can never give them away. Please don't be guilty of that. When you do that, you put a person in a position of not being able to do what God tells them to do with that gift in the future. If you say the person receiving your gift has to do a certain thing with what you have given them, you are still holding on to that thing and still controlling it, even though you have let someone else take hold of it too. That is a gift in name only, for you still own it.

A Foretaste of Glory Divine

That July while campmeeting was going on, a pastor from Australia was preaching. He was telling wonderful stories of things that had happened during his travels and what God was doing among the nations. One night, in the service, the Lord spoke to me to give that pastor the last two remaining pieces of jewelry I owned — two beautiful rings. These rings were very special to me. I had already let go of nearly everything else I owned, except for those rings and my car. I was holding on to these last items. I had bought the car myself, but a friend whom I loved had given me the rings. I knew God wanted me to let go of them, and yet there was that holding on, because they had been given to me by that certain person at that certain time for that certain reason.

I was committed to the Lord and had said to Him, "Everything I have is Yours," and I meant it. I had given away many things already, even things I later needed. For instance, I gave away my broom, thinking I wouldn't need it again. How foolish was that? I gave away my vacuum cleaner, somehow thinking I would never use it again. Still, I held on to those rings and the car.

But one morning I put the rings in my pocket as I left my room, determined to give them to the Australian pastor. Throughout the day I would reach in once in a while and touch them. It was somehow comforting to know that they were still there. I spotted the pastor out walking across the campground, but, instead of going toward him, I turned and went the other way, and my hand was firmly in my pocket.

I went into the camp dining room, and there was a woman in there. She was just a little lady, but a wonderful one, and she had traveled all over the world for God. She was a down-to-earth, plain sort of person, with nothing extraordinary about her appearance. In fact, at this point in her life, she no longer had any teeth. But, oh, she knew how to pray! I went over to her now and asked her to pray for me.

I started to tell her what I needed to make a decision about, but she said to me, "If you want me to pray for you, don't say anything. Don't tell me a thing. Let God see it."

I still had one hand in my pocket on those rings, and when she reached to take hold of my hands, I had to take that one out, and I put them both into her hand. Through her, the Lord said to me that day, "Let go of that which you have in your hands, and do not look back, but put your hands on the plow and plow on with Me, forgetting those things that are behind."

A Foretaste of Glory Divine

By this time, I was weeping, and by the time she finished praying, I had become willing to let go of the things I had been holding on to. Needless to say, there was a great release when I let go of those rings. I didn't have to cherish them anymore, I didn't have to spend time looking at them, and I didn't have to go back and remember the occasion on which they had been given to me. God just washed all of that away and set me free from the past. As long as we hold on to things from the past, when God is dealing with us to let them go, whatever they might be, they become the things that keep us from walking into a greater, more wonderful, and fuller place in Him. Before the day was out, the rings were in the possession of the Australian pastor.

Later that same year, my car went also, and in place of these things, God gave me nations. In place of them, He gave me the souls of men. How foolish I had been to hold on to them and consider them so important and so dear to my life! When I let them go, then God revealed Himself to me in a greater way, so that I could go and take with me His life, His presence, and His power. I could be one who walked among the nations, demonstrating His life and His love for all mankind with healings, deliverances, and many people coming to the Lord. That was worth it all!

Experiencing God's Presence in a New Way

WHEN I FIRST CAME TO THIS campground and was in the meetings, I experienced the presence of God in a way that I had never experienced it before. I had only felt the presence of God once or twice before in my life. I never knew that He could come and take over an entire service and move like a wind.

We experienced it in those early days. The miraculous took place night after night, morning after morning, and afternoon after afternoon. God did miracle after miracle. But it was not just in the tabernacle. We experienced miracles in the dining room, miracles in the kitchen, miracles on the parking lot, and miracles in the snack bar. Miracles happened as we stood in wonder at this mighty God and knew not that there was a preparation taking place in our own lives and our own hearts, that He was taking away things, putting in new things, giving us strength and then letting us walk through a place where we couldn't walk alone and had to call out to Him to help us.

Each of us saw that miracle happen for ourselves, preparing us for a day to come in which we would walk in the power and presence of the Almighty God, anointed and seeing His glory move and bring forth His desires to reap the harvest, to bring forth revival and change. Each of us needs one thing, and that is God, and here at Calvary Campground, we experienced Him every moment of every day and still do these many years later.

One of My Greatest Temptations

ONE OF MY GREATEST TEMPTATIONS, after I had come to live at camp, wasn't something evil, but it was something that God graciously warned me not to do, so in the end, I didn't. I was invited to go back to my old workplace, and the offer was very tempting.

My former employer called to say that if I would come back for just eight weeks to train someone to do what I had been doing, he would give me a wonderful salary. Actually, I *had* trained someone before I left, but when that person found out the hours she would be required to put in on the job, she didn't last long. Being in leadership is not easy. When others are already at rest, you are still on the job, and yet nothing is added to your pay to compensate.

It seems incredible, but I worked more hours than anyone else in the restaurant. I worked long days,

A Foretaste of Glory Divine

sometimes fourteen- to sixteen-hour days, and yet my duties never ended.

I got the telephone call a year after I had left the job, and it came just at camptime. For the next eight weeks, he would provide me a house to live in and pay me ten thousand dollars just to train someone. That sounded really great to me at the time. Just think, I could go and do this for just eight weeks, and I would have ten thousand dollars to help send others around the world that September. That offer sounded so wonderful that I really prayed and sought God about it.

I never got up the nerve to go and tell Brother Heflin what I was thinking, but I had almost made up my mind that this was what I wanted to do. This had to be God, I reasoned! If God was giving me this much money, it must be to go around the world or to send someone else around the world. In the end, I went down to the altar in the tabernacle, and God spoke to me, "If you go, you will become entangled in your work again."

Entangled to me meant that I would be off the path of what He had called me to do and that I wouldn't be able to get back onto that path. *Entangled* meant to me that I would be working again for maybe ten, twelve or fourteen hours a day (like I had my whole life) seven days a week, except for one day off, and if they needed me I would go to work that day too. For so many years I had worked day and night. I went to work at ten o'clock in the morning, got off at two, went back at four thirty and would get home about one or two o'clock in the morning. This was not just for one night, but for every night, year after year after year.

I can honestly say that I loved my job, but when I met Jesus, He changed me, and He gave me something far more wonderful, far more glorious that He had for me. I was walking in that when this invitation came, and thank God, He delivered me from the temptation of leaving it — even for eight weeks.

I am telling all this because nobody seems to understand the concept of serving God by faith today. Your family won't understand it. Your co-workers won't understand it. You will feel as if you are standing on an island all by yourself. I know because I felt that way.

But I wasn't by myself. I was standing in the path of God and His righteousness and was letting Him lead me into something far more wonderful.

Sometimes our families do not understand where we are, what we are doing, where we are going, or what God has called us to. But don't let that stop you. Obedience to God is worth it all — whether anyone else understands you or not.

My First Passport

WHAT A GREAT DAY IT WAS FOR me when my first passport arrived back in the 1970s. Until I had come to camp, I had hardly known that such a thing as a passport existed. I'd had no reason to ever think about a passport, because I had nowhere to go. I had never dreamed of boarding an airplane and going out of the country, and when you have no need of something you never think about it.

One day I overheard someone talking about a passport, and I asked them what a passport was. We sometimes laugh at the ignorance of others, when we're about as ignorant as them. We just know how to keep a straight face about it. There are a lot of things we don't know yet, but we learn by taking steps to do something for God, and, as we take those steps, He honors our faith.

Eventually I realized that I, too, needed a passport and applied for one as soon as possible. It was a step of faith. If I got myself ready, surely God would send me to the nations.

Holy Rolling

WHEN I FIRST CAME TO THE campground in 1976, I saw some strange people doing some strange things, but it was all very wonderful to me. I loved it, and I found that we could all be a little *weird* if we were just willing to open up to God and let Him be God, let Him do something new in our lives, and stop worrying about what our neighbors might think about us. As long as you are worried about what your neighbor will think about you, you will never get anywhere or do anything much for God.

I can tell you how to get rid of that intimidating spirit: go on a forty-day water fast. That will break you forth, break you in, and break you through to something brand new.

But it doesn't even need to be a forty-day water fast. Just go on a forty-day fast, or a thirty-day fast, a twenty-day fast, or whatever the Lord leads you to do. I just happened to be on a forty-day fast, and it was on my fortieth day that I stood at the altar of the tabernacle, and Sister Edith Heflin prayed for me. The words that came out of her mouth were that the Lord was saying, "My power shall surge through your body in a new way." There were many other wonderful things said, but that part stuck in my spirit. I didn't stop fasting that day. I went on to the forty-third day.

That night, we were all line-dancing across the front of the tabernacle, and suddenly the power of God began to surge through my body, and I began to do a new type of dance. I can't describe it, and I couldn't repeat it exactly if I tried, but I couldn't stop.

It was wild. I couldn't fall, I couldn't stand, and I couldn't stop dancing. Eventually, the Lord laid me right down, and I rolled off of the platform and across the front of the tabernacle and kept on rolling. While I was rolling, I rolled through nations, and I saw God at work in each of them.

I saw Him working in Russia; I saw Him working in Mexico; I saw Him doing mighty things in the Philippines; I saw Him at work in China; and I continued to roll through the nations. Today, I can tell you that I have been to all of those nations that I saw that night.

Somebody asked me if I wasn't ashamed of myself for doing that. I said, "Never!" In fact, my thought was: "Do it again, God." And you know what? He did! He did it again, and again, and again, and again, and it was marvelously wonderful.

I considered this to be such a wonderful experience that one year I believed God that every person who worked on my team would roll before the summer camp season was over. I didn't tell them what I was believing for, but I prayed that God would touch them in that wonderful and glorious way.

Every night, after I got off work at the snack bar, usually at about one thirty, I went to the prayer room and danced before the Lord and prayed in the Spirit for the people who were working with me, believing God that He would touch them, and they would roll. And, one-by-one-by-one, in different services, every one of them did.

All, that is, except for one brother. He had been a great worshiper of the Lord until his mom sent him a beautiful pin-striped suit. After he put on that suit, he didn't dance anymore, and he also didn't lift his hands nearly as high. He was just too sharp looking I guess, and he must have been worried that dancing would spoil his look. But if something is holding you back, you'd better get rid of it and let God be God.

I sometimes told the brother that he shouldn't put on his pin-striped suit. He was way too proud of it. I

A Foretaste of Glory Divine

had spoken with his mother the day he had received it, and she was happy to send it to him, but it had not been good for his spirituality.

Toward the end of campmeeting that year, I had already gone up to the snack bar one night when someone came running and said, "You had better come and look at that young man. He has that pin-striped suit on, but he is rolling all over the tabernacle." I wouldn't have missed that for the world, so I went running back down to the tabernacle to see the sight. The young man's arms had come out of the sleeves, and the coat was halfway up over his head, but he was lost in the Spirit, rolling here and there.

That was still in the days when the surface at the front of the tabernacle was rough and very dusty, but the Spirit was rolling that young man over and over again, this way and that, and then every which way. When he finally got up, he went up to the snack bar, but he was still groggy. He leaned up against the wall at the door to the kitchen, then slid down it, and lay down there on the floor for a while.

While he was rolling that night, God spoke to him to give his pin-striped suit to another brother. That other brother had asked him to loan it to him, and he hadn't been willing to do it. Now God told him to give it away.

Lady Jane Lowder

That was not all that God spoke to the young man that night. He told him that he would be going to Israel and would live there for a while. Sure enough, he went to Israel and stayed for a while, working with our fellowship there. He went to Hebrew school, and God gave him the language supernaturally. Today he speaks Hebrew fluently, and it was all birthed in a moment of time, when he allowed God to roll him across the tabernacle floor in his precious pin-striped suit. The result was that he was loosed and set free to do great things for God.

When the Spirit of God comes, anything can happen. Anything! So be open for anything, for God to come your way and touch you in a special, marvelous, and wonderful way.

Things I Didn't Understand

I DIDN'T UNDERSTAND A LOT of the teachings of this camp when I first came here. One of the things I didn't understand was this: I had been making two hundred dollars a week before I came. (Keep in mind that this was in the early 1970s). I said, "God I don't understand this. I quit my job, gave everything away, and I came here, and now I am washing dishes. I sweep floors and do other things I don't really know how to do, like paint, or apply a textured ceiling." (Believe me, I had more paint on me than I had on the ceiling.) I didn't understand it all, but I didn't have to understand it.

Some things I did understand: I knew that God had told me to come here, and I knew that I wanted whatever He had for me. I would give Him time to help me understand it all.

There was a lot I didn't understand about the people I was now working with, like why some of them left a job they were doing and never came back to finish it. I didn't understand why we could go to one job in the morning that was very important, a priority, but by three o'clock that afternoon, the priority had changed, and we were suddenly told to do something else instead. That sounded awfully confusing to me.

But, you see, I didn't see what my leaders saw. I didn't see the importance of things they saw as important. I didn't understand what they understood. I had been taught that when you start a job, you finish it. I had been taught that when it was time for you to get off work, if you had to stay awhile longer to finish the job, you stayed until you finished whatever needed to be finished.

I had been taught to go to work ten or fifteen minutes early, to get there ahead of time, and then to stay on a little longer after normal quitting time. So now I didn't understand some of the things I was being told. But that didn't give me a right or a reason to go down a different path. It didn't give me a right or a reason to find someone and talk about one of our leaders. That didn't give me a right or a reason to speak badly about someone else.

Mother Heflin always told us, "Be sure your sins will find you out," so we always felt that if we did something that was really wrong, before morning she would know about it. Later, I came to understand that God is the One who finds you out. My understanding, because I worked for many years in the world, and we went to work in a natural job and gave ourselves to it: You gave a good day's work in that job.

I was told by our boss, when I worked at a shirt factory for a time, "When you come through that door, drop your problems out there, and when you leave in the afternoon, drop the problems that are in here and pick up your own problems as you go out the door." I understood that advice, and I have always appreciated it. It kept me from bringing problems home and talking about work to others. I learned to just drop them off.

That was in the natural world, but I tell you, as a Christian, we have a bigger and a better drop-off place. Drop it off at the cross. Drop it off at Jesus' feet! Take your burdens to the Lord and leave them there!

I understood about giving a full day's work to my job and to my boss, and when I came here, I gave a full day to my heavenly Boss. His name is Jesus. I never went to my room and laid down. I never purposely made a job last longer than it would normally have taken to accomplish. I tried to do everything as quickly as I could do it and move on to another job. I still do that today. In time, promotion would come.

All Fear Removed

WHEN GOD EVENTUALLY SPOKE to me to go to Egypt alone, my greatest fear was facing Rev. Wallace Heflin, our leader, and asking for his permission to do it. He was very protective of us and didn't want to see any of us fail.

Finally getting up enough courage one day, I went up the stairs to his office, knocked, and went in. "Brother Heflin," I said, "everyone is telling me that you are not going to let me go to Egypt alone. But I must go, for God told me to do it." There, I had said it.

God had spoken to me and told me to go to Egypt by myself, but many of the other leaders in the ministry warned me that Brother Heflin would not let me do it. I understood his reasoning, but I was determined. I had the fear that if God spoke to me to do something, and I didn't do it, my sicknesses could come back on me. I didn't yet know God in the marvelous way I know Him today.

A Foretaste of Glory Divine

Now I know that He doesn't take sickness away from us and then bring it back on us because of something we've done or failed to do. But back then I was afraid.

It took a lot of boldness for me to walk through that office door, more boldness than it took for me to go to Egypt alone. And that's the truth. It was a walk I had to take, and nobody could take it for me.

When I finally came to the end of myself, I said, just as Esther had, "If I die in that office, then I die. And if he says no, then he says no. But I *will* go see him." So I went in and sat down in front of that big desk with that big man sitting behind it.

That big man had such big hands and such big eyes. He was a man I respected, a man I had watched work miracle after miracle. I saw him lay hands on blind people and saw their eyes open. I saw him get people out of their wheelchairs, and I saw God touch them, and they began to walk. I wasn't lacking in respect or honor for the man, but I was afraid not to do what God had told me to do.

My heart was in such a turmoil that I can't remember exactly how I finally got my courage up to go see him. I don't remember if the Lord spoke to me that day, as He often has, "Be of good courage." I just knew I had to do it.

Lady Jane Lowder

Brother Heflin looked up from what he was doing and said, "Yeeeesss, Sister Jane, did you have something you wanted to say?"

I answered, "Yes," and seizing my opportunity, I just blurted out the whole thing.

He had taught us to write out the prophecies we received and then wave them before the Lord, so I had everything written out, each one on a separate sheet of paper. I stood and laid them in front of him, and then I said, "Brother, God has spoken to me to go to Egypt, but everyone is telling me that you will not let me go. You preach, your mother preaches, and other camp leaders preach that if the Lord has spoken to us we must be obedient to do what He says. You can see for yourself what He has told me, but others tell me you still won't let me go."

He didn't say a word, didn't open his mouth, and didn't even raise his eyebrows. He just looked at me. Then he picked up the prophecies and, one by one, read every one of them.

When he had finished, he asked me, "Did God speak to *you* to go?"

I said, "Yes."

He said, "I don't ever tell a person they can't go because I don't want them to go. The only reason I ever question anyone is because I want them to know that they know that they have heard from God. When you get there, and there is nobody else there whom you know, and things don't go the way you thought they were going to go, doors don't open the way you thought they would open, or things don't happen the way you thought they were going to happen, if you are not sure in your own spirit that God told you to go, or it has come from somebody else in a prophetic word, and you don't feel it in your own spirit, then you will accuse them of not being a true prophet, that they have missed it and sent you on a perilous journey.

"Sister Jane, when you know that you have heard from God, when the storm comes, you will be able to stand. You will be able to continue on and work the work that God called you to work. That is the only reason I ever question anyone hearing from God and going forth. I want to know and I want every person to know before they leave that they have heard from God for themselves."

I left his office that day singing a song of victory. I knew that I was going. I knew that I would be able to do what God had spoken to me to do.

I knew that I was going alone. I had heard many people say through the years that God doesn't ever send people out alone, that He sends them out by twos. I, too, often went with other people, either in a larger group or with one or two companions, but this time, for some reason, I felt that I must go alone.

I didn't understand all of this at the time, but now I know why it was so important. I was a very shy person who didn't like crowds. I didn't like to be in the limelight, but preferred staying in the background. God had told me that He would bring me out of hiding. I thought that might be far in the future yet (twenty years or so), but He knows the perfect timing for all things.

When we are open to God, He will accelerate the timetable and begin to do marvelous things for us. Perhaps the most amazing thing is that we suddenly say, "Yes, Lord, I can do that."

Because I would be alone in Egypt, I couldn't depend on anyone else to do the work. I couldn't step behind another and say, "You speak." I couldn't say, "I'll pray for you, and you do the ministry." I had no one else, so I had to do it all. As it turned out, it was not just one meeting a day. It was several meetings each day, and I was forced to get the mind of God for each of them. It was in this way that I began to see God do marvelous and wonderful miracles through me.

I left Brother Heflin's office that day with a much greater confidence. My leader trusted that I had

A Foretaste of Glory Divine

heard from God. From that day until he went home to be with Jesus, I never feared going and talking to him ever again about anything.

I had the kind of respect for Brother Heflin, that if he would have called me at any place in the world and said, "Sister Jane, God spoke to me that you should come home," I would not have questioned him. I would have come home because I knew that he would not tell me to do something unless God had really spoken to him. That particular scenario never happened, but if it had, I would have come without question. As it worked out, God prepared me for the day when I would have to stand alone. I needed that.

Much of the time I was in Egypt I stayed in homes where no one spoke English and only had someone to converse with when an interpreter was present. And when you don't have anyone to compare notes with, you just ask God for His opinion. That, for me, was wonderful!

Egypt was my first I love, and I love her still.

Here, in this place, I was getting more and more of *A Foretaste of Glory Divine*.

Part V

Missionary Stories

God Always Knows Best

GOD DOESN'T ALWAYS SEND US where we expect. For six months one summer I prayed to go to Mexico. Every night, after I had closed the snack bar (anywhere from one to four o'clock in the morning), I walked the campground and prayed, believing for God to send me there. I was so sure that He would do it that I lived Mexico, I loved Mexico, I ate Mexico, and I even rolled Mexico (as I will explain in a moment). Everything I did in those days involved Mexico.

It all started when I rolled off of the platform in the camp tabernacle one night back in the 1970s (as I described in an earlier story). Among the nations I saw that night was Mexico. I rolled up a flag pole, and there was a big sombrero that I unraveled as I was rolling.

During that spiritual adventure, God gave me three words, and I was convinced that they were Spanish words from Mexico. I wrote those words down in the front of my Bible, and I called them out every time I walked the floor in prayer. My thoughts were consumed with Mexico. God was going to send me. I was so sure of it that I would declare, "Mexico, I'm coming."

Then God spoke in prophecy and sent me to China. I loved it, but I thought, "This is not Mexico." Then I went to the Philippines. I loved it, but again I thought, "This is not Mexico." I thought to myself, "How could I have been so wrong?" I had been sure that those three words were Spanish words from Mexico, and I was still determined to walk in them. But I was soon to learn the truth of the matter.

The three words I had thought were Spanish words from Mexico turned out to be the names of places in the Philippines. In that first place, many doors opened to me. When I went on to another place, I discovered that it had the second place name. Those had not just been words, as I had thought; they were actual place names in the Philippines. How amazing that I found myself in the Philippines fulfilling a word that God had given me while I was praying for a totally different country!

To me, those three words sounded Mexican, but I had no way of knowing that, because of its Spanish heritage, many places in the Philippines have

A Foretaste of Glory Divine

Spanish names. The three words were three small villages in the mountains of that country, and I was to meet God powerfully in those places.

Something very important happened in those mountain places. One day, while I was looking down through a beautiful valley, the Lord said to me, "Jane, why don't you call yourself what I call you?"

I said, "I can't. I don't want to."

When Dr. William A. Ward had come into the restaurant in North Carolina one day and spoken a word over me, God had said through him, "I'm going to send you into the nations, and you will travel all over the world preaching My Gospel and bringing salvation, and you will be My evangelist." But, when anyone asked me what I was doing, I would say, "Well, back home at camp I work in the snack bar and the kitchen." I couldn't bring myself to take on the title evangelist. It seemed too great for me.

Even for a time after God had spoken to me there on that mountain and dealt with me to begin saying what He said about me, I still couldn't do it, but it was a beginning. I had met God there, and He put a song in my heart for every coming situation. In time, I would step into the fullness of my calling.

Visiting the Garden of Gethsemane in Taiwan

OTHER CAMP LADIES WERE with me when God sent me to a place in Taiwan called the Garden of Gethsemane. We had meetings there every day for about a week, and the glory of God's presence fell in that place.

It was not a very physically impressive place. It was small, had a dirt floor, and parts of it were surrounded by chicken wire. It was still under construction, and yet, as we gathered there every afternoon about three thirty and prayed, angels came and lined up around the walls.

As I was praying, I saw the Lord high and lifted up in that place, I saw His throne, and I saw Jesus sitting at the Father's side. I also saw people who were gathered unto Him. I had a knowing in my heart that those angels were not just part of a vision. This was real. In fact, it was so real that I went around the building, from angel to angel, thanking them for having come. What a marvelous experience it was!

When God opens your eyes to see the heavenly hosts that have come to be with you, to worship with you, and to carry on the workings of the Lord, *"ministering spirits, sent forth"* (Hebrews 1:14), it is something wonderful indeed.

One day, as we were worshipping, I saw the Lord as He was on His throne, and I saw Jesus sitting next to Him. I saw the people, multitudes of people who were gathered unto Him, and as they were gathered unto Him, I heard and I saw Jesus look over to the Father and say, "Father, these are those whom You have given unto Me. Grant unto them whatsoever they are needing and asking."

I saw God smile and heard Him say, "It is done. It is granted. It is granted!"

There was a young lady there that evening who asked me to pray for her father who was in the hospital. She said, "My dad is not a Christian. He claims to be, but he's not. He beats my mother, and he keeps us from going to church. Now, he's in the hospital, and he is very, very sick, and they say he is not going to make it. Will you pray for him?" I prayed and asked God to send angels to minister to the man that very night.

The lady could not speak English, and the interpreter did not bother to interpret my prayer for her, but she came back the next day and said, "Twelve angels went to my dad's bedside last night and encircled it, and he heard the voice of the Lord speak to him. He called him by his name and said, 'I love you.'"

When the man's wife came to visit the next morning, the first thing he did was repent for the things he had done to her and how he had kept her from attending church services. God totally healed the man and set him free, and, because of this, there was a move of miracles that went through that place.

I went to another place two days later for just one night meeting. There was a woman there who had not spoken for two years. She had also not been able to comb her own hair, give herself a bath, or otherwise take care of herself or her family. All that time she had sat in a stupor, but God totally delivered and set her free that night.

I went back to the Garden of Gethsemane the next morning. We were praying every morning from four to six o'clock, then our first meeting started at eight and wasn't over until about two or three in the afternoon, and we would go back again for the night meeting that ended about twelve midnight or even one A.M. When we went down to prayer that particular morning, I saw something wonderful. Someone had bought carpet and laid it on the dirt floors so that people would have a place to lie in the presence of the Lord and not be on the ground. God began to move on people's hearts to give to that ministry, to give to finish that humble place of worship. The pastor who was over that church is now living in Canada and has a church there.

Moved by a Book

I GAVE BROTHER HEFLIN'S BOOK, *The Power of Prophecy*, to a couple who had been missionaries in Malaysia for many years, and they read it as they were on their three-hour flight back home. They were so touched by the book that they turned around and came back after just one night at home and subsequently invited me to come to their place and preach and teach.

After reading the book, they felt led to repent. Over the years they had received many prophetic words over their lives, but they had not given them much weight. "Perhaps such words came out of someone's overactive imaginations," they thought. There were other prophecies that they *had* considered valid, and they had actually written these down, but they, too, had been set aside and forgotten. Now they got them out and began to re-read them, and were amazed at how many of the things spoken over their lives long ago had already come to pass without them even

A Foretaste of Glory Divine

being aware of it. They were encouraged to use these prophecies as tools in spiritual warfare, and they began to praise the Lord for His promises, believing for the rest of them to come to pass.

My First Three Nations

EARLY IN MY CAMP EXPERIENCE, a wonderful elderly lady from Canada came to minister. She had been a missionary to India for many years. God spoke to me through her and said, "I have given you three nations, and when you have taken those, I will give you three more."

I said, "Lord what are they?" And because I didn't know what the three nations were, it caused me to begin to seek God more to see what He had already spoken to me. Maybe I wasn't listening well enough.

Or, sometimes we don't want to hear what God is saying. We look at ourselves and our inabilities, and we think, "This must be for someone else. God had the wrong person in mind." In this way, we set His promises aside and fail to walk in them.

I began to seek God to know what three nations He had already given me, and He spoke to me that one of them was Egypt, one was the Philippines, and the other was India. When I began to pray about why

A Foretaste of Glory Divine

I had not known this before, I then realized that I might not have been listening well, or had probably dismissed the thoughts because I was looking at the impossibility of me doing any of these things. I didn't yet consider myself to be a preacher or teacher, but God has put ministry within each one of us. When I had finally obeyed God with those three nations, many more were given to me.

Visiting the Bedouins

I HAVE HAD THE PRIVILEGE OF BEING in homes all over the world, many of them of the very poor. In fact, some of the most wonderful times of my life have been in far-away places in the very poor homes of Nepal, India, Pakistan, Thailand, Indonesia, the Philippines, Egypt, and others.

The owners of those homes had little to offer, except for the wonderful love of God and a desire for more of Him. In the Hindu and Moslem countries, Christians often suffer for their faith and have extremely rich testimonies to share.

These were such wonderful times that I can close my eyes and see in vision the faces of the people I met back then, and I remember how God met their need and blessed them. How wonderful!

I have also had the privilege of taking the Gospel into many non-Christian homes. For instance, it was also a wonderful occasion for me when I was able to visit the Bedouins in Eilat (in Israel) and to sit among

A Foretaste of Glory Divine

them and be able to tell them about our wonderful Jesus. They are such wonderful people. As we were going in, they looked at us, and we looked at them. They looked strange to us, and I'm sure we looked strange to them. They didn't speak any English, but I had an interpreter with me who could interpret to a degree. He could not speak their language fluently, but at least he could make conversation with them.

They prepared tea for us, and it was interesting to see how they did it. They first had to build a fire, and then they poured some water into a large tin can and placed it over the heat. Once the water had reached the boiling point, the tea was added, and it was then poured into glasses that had, moments before, been covered with sand. As we watched, they rinsed the glasses in water and then poured the tea into them and served them to us. They watched us while we drank.

After we had finished our tea, they took a bag that had been hanging on one of the tent poles and, from it, began pouring yogurt (we called it clabbered milk at home on the farm). The yogurt was poured into a smaller tin can. This can wasn't smooth at all, but jagged, as if it had been cut with a can opener. This can was then passed around for all to have a sip of yogurt from it. We knew that they were watching us, and some of our people passed it up, but I was not about to. We had been taught that this would be a key to whether or not we were accepted in many parts of the world. Because I drank their yogurt, the Bedouins accepted us, and God did some wonderful things there. We had a very wonderful time sharing with them.

The Bedouin women showed us many interesting things about themselves and their nomadic life. We were able to pray with them, and wonderful things happened. It was the highlight of our time in Israel that particular trip.

Then suddenly, the women heard something. We hadn't heard anything, but they suddenly began to cover themselves ... until all you could see was their eyes. Their men were coming home. As it turned out, the Bedouin women are allowed to show their mouth only to their husbands.

Those were treasured moments. I still pray for that family even today that they will know Jesus without a doubt and follow after Him fully.

Millions of Hindu Gods

IN INDIA AND NEPAL, THE HINDU people have something like thirty-three million gods they worship. They worship everything. Many of their gods are meticulously carved from stone and other materials, and many of their temples are literally covered with these carved images.

Most of the images are not nice at all. They are ugly and vulgar, but they are gods to the Hindu people. Nearly everywhere you go in those countries you can see a big ugly god of stone.

There is a particular look, or stare, in the eyes of these idols, and those who carve them and those who worship them have that same stare. It is easy to see that there is no light in their eyes, no life, and no joy.

I once had a very interesting incident in a humble Indian home. In much of that country, whether the people are poor or not, during the warmer months they go to the rooftops to sleep at night because it is cooler up there. When the family I was staying with got ready to retire to the rooftop that night, the pastor told me I was going to sleep in the house. It was very hot, and there was no fan, but he said they would leave a door and window open to a side terrace. Then he brought me a stick and said, "This is a monkey stick."

I asked, "What do you mean, a 'monkey stick'?"

He said, "If monkeys come in, use this to beat them off."

I thought he was kidding me, and I laughed and laughed. This made him realize that I hadn't taken him seriously, so he took me outside, and showed me that we were right beside a sacred Hindu place of worship. Lo and behold, there was every kind of monkey you could think of. There were monkeys everywhere you looked. The amazing thing is that the people of that place worshipped these monkeys, and if a monkey came into their house and took something, they counted it as a blessing and considered themselves to be highly favored. Thank God we Christians know that a dirty and stinky monkey is not a god.

Well, I got the monkey stick that night, and the rest of the family went to the rooftop, but no monkey dared to come into my room. I wasn't expecting one and didn't want to see one, and so none came. You get what you believe for.

In Nepal the ugly and evil faces of those gods are everywhere. One day of the year, the Nepalese worship dogs, but all the rest of the year dogs are not treated very well there. Poor things!

Ducks are also considered to be gods. Cows are supreme, and they wander down the streets of India and Nepal and do whatever they want to do. At one time, if you killed a cow, even accidentally, your life would be taken.

In Nepal, there is one particular temple where the entire nation gathers once a year to worship a variety of gods and give them animal sacrifices. Even though the people are so poor, their gods are often covered with gold. Their places of worship are often adorned with gold. Even the roofs are covered with gold. This is not something that just *looks* like gold; it *is* real gold. These temples are often held up by four evil-looking serpent carvings.

In these places of worship, hundreds and even thousands of people stand in line with their animal sacrifices to bring to the gods that inhabit those particular temples. Their belief, however, is that the animal must first give its consent. The animals are ready for sacrifice, if, after having water flicked on them, they shudder. This is taken as them giving their permission to be sacrificed.

After gaining the animal's permission, it is sacrificed, and its blood is poured on one or more of the gods honored in that place. The people have to haggle with the priests for them to do their priestly duties, and then, when all is said and done, they can take the meat home to eat. Sometimes they wash it in the stream and cook it right there and have a picnic. How sad their lives are!

As I watched, I thought to myself, "These people, who know not the Living God, who have no salvation and no heart change inside of them, travel for days and then stand in line for hours and hours to get to the place to offer a sacrifice, and we, who know Jesus, who is the Living Sacrifice for us, often don't even want to come to an altar to spend a few minutes with the One who gave His life for us.

It was such a privilege to bring the Gospel to these people. Praise God that we Christians have the real Christ, the Lamb of God, the sacrifice for our sins!

Standing on the Inside

ON ONE OF MY VISITS TO ISRAEL, I became very ill with hepatitis and went through a difficult struggle physically. My body ached, my back ached, and I felt like I was being pulled to pieces.

Our whole team was praying every morning from eight to noon, and we never sat down during all that time. There were chairs to sit on, but nobody sat. Except for one fifteen-minute break, we stood the whole time.

On top of that, it was wintertime, and most of the houses in Israel didn't have any heat. We had a little bit of wood, and so we made a fire each morning to take the chill off of the room. At one point during the prayer time, I got so cold that I went over and sat down by the fire. Sister Ruth Heflin, who headed that ministry for so many years, looked over at me and said, "It's all right to sit down on the outside, as long as you are standing up on the inside." That was a revelation to me, and I've tried to follow that rule ever since.

Going to Washkagginish

WASHKAGGINISH ... WHEN I WENT there, there was no road going in, except what they called the winter road, and in the summer time, there were no roads whatsoever. You went in either by plane or by boat. It was probably one of the most exciting trips I ever made, and we had many miracles on that trip, miracles for our travel, for our vehicles, and for ourselves personally.

This primitive tribal place is located in a very secluded area of Canada, and there were not many people coming in or going out. You couldn't run down to a WalMart or to any of the fast-food restaurants. There was one general store when I was there, and that was it. But, oh, God did miracles in that place!

God Saved a Witch Doctor

IN THE PHILIPPINES, I ACTUALLY went to the house of a witch doctor. His wife was very ill, and so he asked us to come there and conduct a service and pray for her. We went in force — fourteen of us altogether.

As a result of that meeting, the man's wife got saved. She had been so ill that she could walk only with the help of a cane. For some reason, her body was bent over, and she couldn't straighten up.

We preached that day from the Word: *"For God so loved the world, that he gave his only begotten Son, that whosoever believeth in him should not perish, but have everlasting life"* (John 3:16). She accepted Jesus as her personal Savior. When I prayed for her, she was slain in the Spirit, and while she was on the floor, God filled her with the Holy Ghost. When she eventually got up, she was straight, healed by the power of God.

As for her husband, he didn't receive anything that day. When the meeting got underway, he left the house. However, I am happy to report that he, too, got saved a few weeks later. His son also got saved. God did some wonderful things for the whole family.

Carrying a Sister with a Broken Leg

WHILE WE WERE TREKKING with a group through the Himalayan Mountains in Nepal, one of our young ladies fell and broke her leg. Those mountain paths were so steep that we could look down thousands of feet. It was treacherous going under any conditions, but now we had this to deal with.

It was too far to go back, so from there on, we had to carry our sister (and she was not a small person). The path was all up and down steep mountain trails, and we couldn't put her down. We carried her until nightfall every night. Someone else had to carry the extra backpacks, along with their own. We did this for the next five days.

On one of those days, she was carried piggyback (by one of the young Nepali men), from eight o'clock in the morning until sundown, and on the rest of the days she was carried on a stretcher between two persons. It was a terribly trying time for us all, but we met God in the midst of it. Soon after she fell and broke her leg, we began to sing a song of praise unto the Lord as we walked, and God strengthened us.

We stopped and took a drink of water and then rested a little while in a dry river bed. There were no stores anywhere near at hand and no way to get anything. There were no Coca-Colas, no cold water, and we couldn't stop to get anything to eat. What we had brought with us was all that we had.

Our Nepali friend had told me, before we left the capital city, that the man who was carrying the lady with the broken leg used to speak in tongues but had stopped, so I used that opportunity, while he was kneeling down resting, and said to him, "Look up! The Lord wants to fill you with the Holy Ghost, and when you start speaking in other tongues, she will not seem nearly as heavy."

No sooner had I prayed for the brother than he started speaking in other tongues. He spoke and spoke and spoke until his eyes were flowing (just as his nose was flowing, and his mouth was flowing). By the time he had finished speaking in tongues, he had found a new strength in God, and he picked up his burden to go on to the next mountain.

A Foretaste of Glory Divine

In the midst of all of this, we found God, we found a song, we found a praise, we found a worship, and we kept on finding God in wonderful ways.

Trekking for the Gospel

TO REACH FAR MOUNTAIN VILLAGES in Nepal, we would leave the capital city at eight thirty in the evening by car and drive to the end of the road, arriving about five the next morning. There we would wait for daybreak to come to start hiking. There was no other way to get there.

One particular time, when we did this, we walked from about seven in the morning, as soon as it started getting daylight, and we kept walking all day long. By evening, we had crossed the same river nine times. At some crossings the water was only knee deep, but at others it was much deeper. What became challenging was protecting the guitar I had brought along to accompany the music in the meetings we would hold in the village.

One of the brothers held it high in the air as we crossed the river. It was well worth the effort, for the people of that place had never heard a guitar played before.

A Foretaste of Glory Divine

We had traveled all night and then walked all day, but now we had a meeting starting about eight o'clock that evening, and the meeting lasted until past midnight. The anointing of God will give you strength to keep on keeping on in the midst of any struggle. These mountain people were so hungry that they would have stayed there until morning if we had been willing (and physically able) to continue the meeting.

One of the Nepali brothers was praying that I would leave the guitar behind when we left the country, and he was so happy when God told me to do just that. He said he had prayed that guitar out of me.

During this time, other groups of believers trekked the Himalayas in an attempt to take the Gospel to those previously unreached villages, but not everyone was successful. Many set out, but found the climbing too physically taxing and, after a day or two, turned around and went back. God was gracious to us and kept us moving, ministering, and giving out copies of the gospels in the local languages as we went.

We later received a report about a young man who had walked for ten days to get to Kathmandu. He had received a copy of the Gospel of John through one of those treks and wanted to see if there were more copies available. He had read it himself and thought it was so wonderful that he had then gone to every house in his village and read it to his neighbors. Many of them had gotten saved as a result.

He had never been to Katmandu, but now he walked all the way there to see if someone had more of those wonderful books. It was only after he got there that he learned about the existence of Matthew, Mark, and Luke, as well as many other wonderful books of the Bible that he hadn't known about. His whole village was saved from that one small book.

We don't know who gave out that particular Gospel of John, but somebody hand carried it to that far mountain village, and that young man is to be congratulated for having had the burden to take it house to house and read it to his neighbors.

On another of those trips, our strength was tested to the max when our Nepali guide took us the wrong way. Either he had never been there before, or there had been a landslide, and the previous trail had been covered over. Whatever the case, we found ourselves on the wrong side of the mountain looking down. Before that trip was over, I lost four toenails, and we had to make every effort just to get to the next tree. We eventually got to our destination, but by then we were literally crawling on our hands and knees. A man from the village came down to meet us and later told his people he had found us on all fours.

We were supposed to have arrived there the day before, and that man had given up on us and had asked the question: "Why do Christians lie?" Then, when we showed up the next day, having made such a heroic effort to get there, he was delighted and told us he had to repent because he had called us liars.

In that village, all the children had boils. I picked up one child and put him on my lap. He had a big boil on the side of his leg and other boils on his neck and head. One child had a boil that covered the entire top of his head.

The reason so many children had boils was that the villagers had so little water. It would take them all day just to get enough drinking water for themselves and their animals. And that was far more important to them than bathing. The result was these boils.

I had just a little tube of Neosporin with me (which does nothing at all for boils). I took a little of that ointment now and put it on the boy's leg, thinking it might bring him a little comfort. When I looked up, all the mothers were standing in line with their children, and they all wanted some of this salve I had for their boils.

Lady Jane Lowder

I tried to tell them, through a Nepali brother, that the salve I had would not do anything at all for the boils. It couldn't heal them, but it might make them feel a little bit better. "But," I said, "I know a Man who healed me. I will put some salve on your boils, but then I would also like to tell you about this Man. Just as He healed me, I believe He will heal your children of their horrible boils."

One by one, I held those children in my lap and put some of that Neosporin on them. One young man had boils in his ear. When I pressed on his ear pus would shoot out of it.

I also had some peroxide with me, and I poured some of that into his ear. Before long, I was pouring peroxide into everybody's ears.

Eventually we were able to preach the Gospel there. I can't say what all happened in that village after we left, but I know for a surety that the power of God's Word and His love went forth from that village (from the man we had gone to meet).

That first night, when we went to bed, the men were to sleep on the porch, and we ladies were to sleep in the house. I was on the floor, and other ladies were sleeping on a table. After a while, the owner came in, lit a paper torch and moved it up and down the walls. Being from the farm, I understood what he was doing. We used to do the same thing back home. He was trying to get rid of chicken mites.

One of our ladies used hearing aids, and she took them out for the night. After a while, our guide called out to me, "Do you feel something crawling on you?"

"Yes," I said, "it's chicken mites."

The sister with the hearing aids didn't hear that, and the next morning she said, "You know, the strangest thing happened to me last night. I have never had the sun affect me in this way before. It felt like something was walking on me or crawling on me all night long." I had to tell her that it wasn't the sun; it was chicken mites.

God did wonderful things as we went from village to village and from place to place in those remote mountains. Another thing we carried with us was the Bible on tape, and we gave these sets to many of the village leaders. Then we had to leave them in the hands of God.

The Toughest Women in the World

I BELIEVE THAT THE WOMEN OF Nepal and Tibet have to rank among the toughest in the world. In those areas, you can see what looks like a tree walking up the road, and you discover that, under all that load, is a little woman, carrying kindling back home for her family because there is no tree growth in the higher elevations.

One of the things that impressed me so much about the Nepali women was their dedication in going out very early every morning to gather whatever they need for the day, for themselves and their animals. By eleven in the morning, they would be back to attend our service that lasted until one or two o'clock, during the heat of the day. By three in the afternoon, it was already getting cold and people were preparing for the night.

A Foretaste of Glory Divine

In one place, we slept in a goat shed, and when we woke up in the morning, the women of the village were waiting to be prayed for, before we had even started our day. What women! That whole village got saved.

Battling the Heat in India

ONE YEAR, WHEN I WAS IN INDIA, it was one hundred and forty degrees during the day, and it didn't cool off much at night. At four o'clock one morning, I asked the Lord, "I know You said *'the sun shall not smite thee by day,'* but what do You have to say about this heat?"

I got up, picked up a concordance I had with me, and looked up heat. Sure enough, in Isaiah, it said this: *"Neither shall the heat nor sun smite them"* (Isaiah 49:10). I said, "That's my promise," and I danced all over that room with that word lifted up unto the Lord.

That terrible heat never bothered me from that moment on. I was able to keep on going, and the locals thought I was "something" because they were bothered greatly by it themselves.

I haven't experienced terrible depths of cold yet, but I met a woman in China who was sent to Siberia as a prisoner for her faith in the Lord Jesus Christ. They took away her warm coat and her shoes and gave her a hoe and told her to go out and break up the frozen ground. She had to do it barefooted. She told us that while she was out there, the Lord Jesus came and stood beside her and warmed her body so that the cold would not kill her. She had been in that prison for twenty long years and yet she said, "I am ready to go back again for my faith in Jesus." What a testimony!

Alone and Unable to Communicate

EARLY IN MY MISSIONARY experience, I spent a lot of time in Taiwan. Few of the people around me spoke English, and I was always by myself in the daytime and only had an interpreter when I was speaking or praying over people. Every morning I would go to prayer with the Bible students, even though we couldn't communicate with each other. I will never forget what happened one morning.

During prayer that morning, one of the students came over to me, laid their hand on my shoulder, and prayed for the longest time. This was not just a "God-bless-her" prayer. This person prayed seriously and earnestly.

I had my face down on a chair, so I didn't know who it was who was praying for me and was not even sure if it was a man or a woman. What I did know was that as this person prayed, something heavy lifted off of me. I wasn't sure exactly what it was, maybe something I had been trying to pray through. I had been going from service to service, sometimes two or three services a day, speaking and ministering, and not having anyone to talk to in between, but God knows what we need and will often lead us to lay our hands on others and pray.

That person who prayed for me did not speak a single word that I understood, and yet when they prayed, God lifted a burden off of my life. When I got up from there, I got up with a song in my heart, a delight in my soul, and a joy for going on to the service that day.

We might not know what someone needs, and we need not always be seeking a word over their lives, but you can even silently lay your hands on them and pray to the Lord, since He is the One who lifts burdens, the One who answers prayers.

Left Alone to Minister

WHEN I WENT TO INDIA THE first time it was with Brother Heflin and a group of other people. I was scared to death, but I stuck close to the others.

Every night one group would go out to the various villages and have meetings, and another group of us would stay behind and have meetings in a huge driveway in front of Dr. Joshua Raj's house. The meetings started out rather small, but increasingly large numbers began to come until the street was filled with them.

Every night, as the Word of God was preached, wonderful things happened, as the light of His glory would shine upon us. Sometimes we didn't feel anything other than the burdens of the people. We felt as if we were pressing through something all the time. Each of us would have a long line of sick and afflicted to pray for, and we had to make a line for them to stay behind as they waited their turn.

A Foretaste of Glory Divine

Otherwise they would press in upon us because they were so eager.

Because God was doing such great miracles, one night the people were pulling on my sari until they had nearly pulled it off of me. One of the Indian sisters had to come over and wrap me back up.

Brother Heflin and the other team finished their meetings, and came back to prepare to go on to Nepal. He asked if anyone in the group felt led to stay behind in India. I said I did, so I was left. Two more of our sisters were still out in the village, and I wanted to go there and meet up with them. At least, that was my plan. I had no idea that I was about to become the speaker to continue the meetings with Dr. Raj.

As the group was preparing for their flight to Kathmandu, Brother Heflin said to me that it was not too late to change my mind and go on with them. I said, "No, I'm going to stay."

When they had boarded their flight, Dr. Raj didn't waste any time putting me to work. He turned to me and said, "Come with me." He then had me pray for all of the airport personnel on duty that day. We were there until noontime as one-by-one they came to me for prayer.

I didn't have a problem with that. I was used to praying for people and enjoyed it, especially when the Lord gave me a word to speak over their life. This made the experience easier for me and more rich for them. I was comfortable with it because that was what we had been taught, and I had given many such words.

But, then, when we got back to Dr. Raj's house, there were about two hundred and fifty to three hundred people sitting in his yard. Surprised, I asked him what they were doing there. He said, "They are waiting for you."

Wow! That scared me to death. I thought, "What am I going to do with these people?"

I told him I needed to go into the house for a minute but that I would be back. What could I do? I suppose I could have run away, if I could have found somewhere to run to. The thought crossed my mind. I suppose I could have told Dr. Raj that I just couldn't do it, but that wasn't what we had been taught. We had been taught to open ourselves up and let God use us when there was an opportunity.

Thank God for the Holy Ghost and His continual encouragement and strength. I ran up to the bathroom, closed myself in, and prayed. I said, "God, these are not *my* people; they're *Your* people. You have got to give me something to speak to them, and I need it right now, because I don't know what to do, what to say, or how to say it."

As I was going into the house, Dr. Raj had pointed out to me that there was a young man there who had been deaf and dumb from birth. Cases like that have a way of dominating your thoughts. The devil tries to use it to make you think it is your responsibility to heal them, and it puts a great pressure on you, when, in reality, it has nothing to do with you at all. All God is asking of us is to open up the treasure chest that is within our earthen vessels and let the power of His presence and the glory of who He is begin to flow out from us in the way He desires it.

All God is asking us to do is to yield our vessel to Him and let Him fill us and then to speak the words (and only the words) He gives us to speak. We can forget about ourselves and turn the eyes of the people upon Jesus, in whom all the answers for their lives are to be found. It's not about you or me; it's about Him.

Still shaking in my boots, I took my place in that crowd. I cannot tell you where I read from that day, and I cannot tell you what I spoke. I can't even tell you what the crowd looked like because I closed my eyes so that I wouldn't see them, and I kept my eyes closed the whole time I was speaking. I remembered

Dr. William A. Ward saying, "Don't look upon their faces," so I didn't look.

As my message was coming to a close, the thought came to me, "I'm going to do this just like Brother Heflin does. I'm going to have a call for those who need to get saved, then I'll pray for the sick, and, finally, I will invite those who desire to receive the Holy Ghost. I did that.

When I finally opened my eyes, I was amazed to see many of the people weeping, both men and women. I thought, "Oh, God, I probably did something very bad to offend them." But that was not the cause of the commotion at all. It was the young man who had been born deaf and dumb. He had been totally healed and set free.

It was a marvelous time, as many were saved, many were healed, and many were filled with the Holy Ghost. When it was all over I was wonderfully happy in the Lord ... for about fifteen minutes. No sooner had we sat down to eat than Dr. Raj said, "There is another meeting tonight at eight in the Methodist Church." I would have given anything if he hadn't said that until I had finished eating, because now all of that fear rose up in me again. I had to somehow find another message for that night.

A Foretaste of Glory Divine

All afternoon I prayed and sought the Lord. I told Him, "You said that in this earthen vessel is a treasure of Your life, a treasure of Your Word, and a treasure of Your giftings. I'm asking You, Lord, to help me open up the treasure chest and let what is inside it flow out tonight." That was the night that God changed my heart and my mind and made me to know that I would not be spending my immediate future in America. I would keep on going and going, and God would be with me anywhere I went to confirm His Word with signs following.

Again, I can't tell you what my Bible text was that night, or what exactly I preached. What I can tell you is that when I opened my eyes at the end of the message and made an altar call for those who wanted to be saved, hundreds of people flooded forward and stood around the altar praying. When I called for people who needed healing, they came and got healed. And when I prayed for those who wanted to receive the baptism of the Holy Spirit, they came and received.

Before making this final call, I had asked everybody to go back to their seats, and they had. Now, as I began making the call, the people were so eager that they began to receive as they got up to come. Before they reached the front, many were already speaking in tongues. I never got to lay my hands on any of them, and I prayed for no one in particular that night. Jesus was so wonderful, so real, and so powerful that I watched from the platform as His presence and power moved through those people, touching them, healing them, making them whole, and filling them with His Spirit. In those moments, I had a knowing which has never left me to this day, that God didn't need me, but that He had chosen to use me for His glory. He could do it all by Himself, but He was giving me the privilege of being part of what He wanted to do.

Another realization came over me that night: If God could bring revival like this in India, He could do it anywhere in the world He chose to send me. Wherever it happened to be that I preached His Word, He would be there to reveal His signs and wonders and meet the needs of the people.

In the years ahead, the Lord would give me many opportunities to go and preach and see His power and glory revealed at the preaching of His Word, as thousands were saved and delivered, all to His glory.

I still don't know how to do it today, but He knows how to do it, and He will do it in your life, too.

Letting God Use Her

I HAD THE GREAT PRIVILEGE OF traveling for many years with one lovely lady named Mary Wagner. When Mary came to camp, she felt that God wasn't doing much in her life, that He wasn't using her in any significant way, and that she didn't have as much to offer as others.

When I traveled with anyone, I always insisted that they let God use them, that they prophesy and bless the people wherever we went. I kept pushing this woman in this way, but she felt that she had little to offer. Then one day, while we were ministering in the Philippines (I can't remember if it was in Iloilo City or Bacolod), suddenly she opened her mouth and began to prophesy, and that released the floodgates.

Two days before that I had said to her, "Sister, I don't know what this means, but God shows me that you are going to be weeping like a weeping willow tree."

She said, "Well that *would* be a miracle because I haven't wept in forty years or more. I can't cry at all." That day, when she opened her mouth and that prophetic river began to flow out of her belly, I looked out at her, and tears were streaming down her face. She later told me that she considered the tears to be as much of or even a greater miracle than the prophetic words coming out of her mouth. She got two great miracles in one day.

Mary still was not satisfied that she was growing in God as she should, so one day I asked the Lord what I could do or say to her to make her realize how she was growing. Many of us become discouraged when we don't see enough change in ourselves. God showed me a picture of a hand. The fingernails were very shapely, and then I saw them grow, and they became unshapely. God spoke to me and said, "Ask her if she can see her fingernails growing?" I asked.

Her answer was simply, "You know I can't!"

"Well," I told her, "the Lord is saying that your spiritual growth is just like your fingernails. You can't see them growing, but every once in a while you have to reshape them because they have grown. Know also that, in the very same way, you are growing, and He is shaping you." I'm very grateful for the many years I had to travel with that great lady. In 1999, she went on to her reward.

A Sight to Behold

ONCE, WHEN I WAS TRAVELING with a team by ship in Greece, a sudden storm arose at sea, and the ship's staff came around passing out little paper boxes. These reminded me of the paper boxes the Chinese fill with rice, but in another way, they looked like the old paper boxes we used for ice cream.

One of our sisters, an elderly lady in her late seventies or early eighties, was asleep when the staff brought the boxes out, so they just put one on her lap. The storm had not been so bad when they first brought them around, but they had foreseen something that we could not. When our sister woke up and saw everyone holding those boxes, she thought they had passed out ice cream and she had missed it. The boxes, however, had another purpose. They were to collect as much of the vomit as possible.

The ship was now tossing in the sea, and I had many people telling me how not to get sick. "Walk

Lady Jane Lowder

with you head straight up and keep on walking, only looking forward." That was just one of many methods I heard that day. Others had more sound advice. One person, for instance, said, "Brace yourself."

Well, I got sick anyway, and I do mean sick. In fact, most everyone on the boat that day was sick. Some people were sitting, some lying against the walls. The bathroom was a sight to behold. Believe me, we needed the boxes. But God keeps us through all sorts of circumstances.

"Walk Down This Road"

ONCE, WHEN A GROUP OF US were out in the Australian outback, the Lord told us to walk down a certain road, and as we walked, a man came along carrying a child on his shoulders. It was apparent that the child could not walk, so we stopped the man and asked him what was wrong.

He said his child had not walked from the time of her birth (and she was then about three and a half or four years old). We told him we were going to pray, and we believed that God was going to heal that child. He took her off of his shoulders, we prayed for her, and God healed her, and she started walking that day. We went and had church in that man's house, and his child was the center of attention because she was walking.

The next morning there was a man lying out in the yard. He couldn't get up, to knock on the door, so we prayed for him, and he got up. God does such wonderful things!

Accept God's Timing

ONE YEAR ANOTHER SISTER and I had a wonderful plan. We would leave Virginia in October or November to travel in ministry overseas and not come back until the next May. It was a great plan, but just before we left, God spoke to me and told me to come back in February instead, and He told me exactly what day in February to come back.

That didn't fit our great plan, and I really didn't want to do it, because I had already advertised ministry in other places. So I went to the other sister and asked her if God had shown her anything about coming back early. She said, "No."

I said, "You need to pray because God spoke to me about coming back early, even though I really didn't want to hear it."

Whenever God speaks to you to do something, change your plans. He will not remove you from one place just for the sake of removing you or causing you trouble. Rather, He always has a greater plan in mind for you.

A Foretaste of Glory Divine

Later that year, we were having meetings in Taiwan, and I called home to ask one of the sisters here at camp to call my brother and check on my mom for me and then call me back and let me know how she was. She never returned the call, so I figured that Mom was okay. But because God told me to go home, our meetings were cancelled, and we left the place we were and went to Taipei, the capital, and caught a plane out.

On the plane coming back to the U.S., somehow the thought came into my spirit that my mother had died. I pushed that thought aside and reasoned in my mind that it could not be possible. If her condition had worsened or she was in danger, someone would have called me and told me. Still, the thought of her dying was so real to me that I considered telling my traveling companion about it, but since I reasoned that it could not possibly be true, I held my peace.

Actually the other sister had a dream on the plane that my Mom had died, but she didn't tell me because she didn't want me to worry me about it. When we got to the airport in Richmond, one of the camp sisters was there to pick up us. She greeted us and didn't say anything else until we were in the car. When we got in the car, I noticed a note to her that said, "Call Jane's brother James," so I asked her, "How's my Mom?"

Her surprising answer was, "She passed away just five hours ago."

God had known what would happen, and He had changed my plans back in November, before I ever left camp, and told me to be on that plane that day to come back home. When I got back, Mom had already gone on to be with Jesus. If we had insisted on going on to the places we had been planning to visit, my family would never have been able to get in touch with me because, in some of those places, communication was very limited. God is so faithful. Trust Him.

Egypt, My First Love

SOME OF THE HAPPIEST MOMENTS in my life have been passed in Egypt, a place where I met God and met His people in a brand new and glorious way. It was to Egypt that I took my first missionary journey alone. God had spoken to me and told me that I was to go and that I was to go alone.

I was just a country girl, not knowing very much, but there was one thing I knew: Jesus had said to me, "If you will go and tell about Me, I will go with you, and I will confirm My Word with signs and wonders." He had saved me, given me new lungs, a new stomach, a new life, new joy, new breath, and if He had done all that for me, I knew that He could do it for others as well. Oh, I had a wonderful time in Egypt!

Brother Heflin had given me the name and address of an Egyptian pastor. He had not heard from this pastor in a while and couldn't be sure that he would still be living at the same address, but I found that in Egypt people don't move nearly as often as we do here in America. Just in case, Brother Heflin gave me the name of a hotel in Cairo where I could stay one night, while trying to get in touch with the pastor. If, for some reason, I was unable to get in touch with him, I was on my own. But God did a wonderful thing.

Even though I got to the hotel about two or three o'clock in the morning, I got up early the next day to try to contact this local pastor, and I was able to get him on the telephone. Then, about the time I began to tell him who I was and where I had come from, the phone line went dead, and it stayed dead for the next eight hours.

I sat in the hotel all day long, every few minutes going and dialing that number. When I finally got in touch with the pastor again, he invited me to come to his house. Oh, how wonderful that invitation seemed to me in that moment!

Since Cairo was so strange to me, the pastor gave the directions to his house to the hotel manager, and the hotel manager gave the directions to a taxi driver. For my part, as the taxi pulled away from the hotel that day, I didn't have a clue as to where I was going. There were other people in the taxi, and some of them were drinking, and I wasn't so sure about the whole thing, and whether or not I would get to my destination safely.

A Foretaste of Glory Divine

Cairo's streets, at three or four in the afternoon, are very crowded, and that car didn't seem to be making much headway. I wasn't even sure if they were taking me to the right place. But I had no choice but to sit there, not really knowing what was happening and putting my trust in a taxi driver I had never seen before in my life. I had a note in my hand with the pastor's address on it, but otherwise this was a totally new experience for me, and I wasn't really sure about how it would turn out

It took us a very long while, because of the heavy traffic, but finally I arrived at the place. The pastor's daughter came out to greet me. Her father wasn't there, she said, but he would be coming soon, and she helped me to become comfortable in their home. In the days ahead, that man became like a father to me, and he opened many wonderful doors for my ministry.

He was a great man of God in his own right. In fact many called him "Little Jesus." He started out every morning about nine o'clock, right after breakfast, making house calls. I would go with him, and he would allow me to pray for the people we met. This not only opened doors for me, but as I stepped through those doors, God began to do new things in and through me.

Lady Jane Lowder

It was in Egypt that I began to move in the Word of Knowledge, and it was in Egypt that I began to see God heal and set men and women free through my ministry. Through me, He began to awaken people's hearts. Many got saved, many were healed, and many were filled with the Holy Ghost.

I had another wonderful interpreter, also a pastor and a wonderful man of God, and he traveled with me everywhere I went. I was in Egypt that first time for about six weeks, and God did many great things there. The Egyptians I traveled with named me "The Iron Woman" because I never took a nap in the afternoon, as they were accustomed to doing.

One of the most wonderful miracles I saw the Lord do in Egypt on that trip was in Alexandria, close to the end of my time in the country. I went to a church which was packed out (you almost couldn't move), and as I was ministering in that place, there was a young man sitting in the corner. As I was speaking, God told me to tell him that the person who was persecuting him would not persecute him anymore, the one who had been giving him problems would not give him problems anymore. God said, "I am delivering you." That brother started weeping, and he cried and cried.

While he was still weeping, another man jumped up and said, "I'm that man who has been bothering him," and he gave his heart to Jesus. He was saved, filled with the Holy Ghost, and got his life turned around. What a marvelous thing it was!

It was in Egypt that I spoke to a certain young man one day. His dad was the custodian of the church, and he asked me to come pray for all his children. As I was going around the room praying for them, I came to one young man who said, "I don't want you to pray for me."

I said, "Okay, I won't," and I kept on praying for others.

When we finished and I got back to the front, I looked back at him, and I heard these words come out of my mouth, "You will not sleep another night until you come to know the Lord Jesus Christ." That was all that God said on the subject, and the meeting continued.

We had another meeting the next night, and when we got to the church there was a note on the podium for me to go and see that young man. I didn't have time that next day, and the next night there was another note there saying, "Please, if you can, come to my house after the service. I cannot sleep." We went to the young man's house, which was close by, and prayed for him. He got saved, got filled with the Holy Ghost, and then traveled with me for many weeks, opening many other doors. We ministered to all of his friends. We would get out of a meeting at eleven or twelve o'clock at night and then go out on house calls, praying for people in their homes. We did this night after night. In the afternoons, we also made house calls, praying for people wherever we found them hungry and open to God.

One day, as we were visiting a man's father on a second story, a lady followed us up the stairs. We were told that she was a prostitute. The man we were sent to visit couldn't walk because he was unable to put any weight on his right foot. He had been in this condition for a long time. I said to him, "I believe. I am going to pray for you, and then you are going to get up, and you are going to walk. Jesus is going to heal you."

While I was telling him about Jesus and about the power of Jesus to heal, the lady from downstairs sat nearby and laughed and made fun of what I was saying, but God helped me to tune her out. I prayed for him and said, "Now, get up. You can walk."

He got up and started walking, then he began to bang his foot on the floor. With this, the women sitting nearby began to weep.

God had healed the man's foot, and while I was talking to him and while he was walking, God had

A Foretaste of Glory Divine

given me a vision for her. He showed me her back and what was wrong with it and how much pain she was suffering in her body. I turned to her and said, "God says to tell you that He will heal you also." The power of God came upon that woman, and God healed her, taking all the pain out of her body. She also got saved. Oh, what a wonderful first trip I had to Egypt!

Planting Rice Brings Salvation

WHILE THREE OF US WERE ministering in the Philippines, I felt the Lord telling me that we should go out with the people into the rice fields that day and plant. None of us had ever planted rice before, and when we got into the rice field, we found ourselves standing in mud up over our knees. We didn't know what the Lord was doing, but we trusted Him.

Later, we were invited to the landowner's home for lunch. They served us beans and rice. We were asked to say a blessing over the meal, and the pastor whispered to me, "Pray the whole thing, with complete salvation in it."

I prayed a very complete prayer that day, including salvation for the owners, and the woman and her husband were saved, and many others were touched and God healed them and set them free.

A Foretaste of Glory Divine

That night she came to the church and came and sat on the platform with us. It all happened because we were obedient to go out and help plant rice.

With Little in Our Pockets

ONE YEAR, THREE OF US LADIES from camp left together after camptime to make an around-the-world missionary trip. We had our plane tickets, but otherwise we had less than eighty dollars each. Two of us had only half of our ticket paid. Brother Wallace Heflin, being the great father of faith and encourager that he was, had helped us to get our tickets and allowed us to pay the rest later.

Actually someone had given me the money for my full fare, but since I knew that one of the other ladies didn't have hers, I gave her half of what she needed, so that we could all get started. So off we went to go around the world, with half a ticket paid and about seventy two dollars each.

That might sound to some like we didn't have very good sense, but it doesn't take a lot of sense to follow Jesus. You just have to know how to say yes to Him. And if you have too much of what some call "sense," you can talk yourself out of doing things, because sense will tell you not to risk it. But truly good sense is following Jesus, wherever He leads.

On our way across to the West Coast, we visited several churches here in America, and they gave us offerings, but we sent that money back to camp to pay on our tickets.

Then, when we got to Hawaii, God did a wonderful thing. We didn't know anyone there, so we looked in the Yellow Pages under churches. There were, of course, quite a few pages full of churches to choose from. We prayed over those pages, asking the Lord which one of those places we should go to, and finally decided to go to one called Prayer Mountain.

On our way to the place, one of the sisters had a vision and saw the head table of that ministry. There was a plate laid at the head position on the table, but the chair for that space was leaning up against the table. She said to us, "The Lord is showing me that the head of this ministry we're going to is not there." We weren't worried. We knew we had made a good decision.

When we arrived at Prayer Mountain, sure enough, we were told that the head of the ministry was not there. Furthermore, he had left unnoticed, not telling anyone where he was going, and he had now been gone for a long time, and nobody knew exactly where he was. This didn't dampen our enthusiasm at all. We had a wonderful time in that place anyway, as we were warmly received. We also ministered in a house meeting.

During our time in Hawaii, the Lord gave us about five hundred dollars, and we sent it all back to camp to go on our tickets. Then we soon began our journey outside of the United States.

Moving around Korea and Japan, it was not long before our money was nearly gone. We had learned that there was an airport tax to be paid upon leaving, and we knew that we would have some motel costs, so we didn't eat much at all during our stay there. In each place, the Lord led us, and we found places to minister, hungry hearts who were eager to hear of Him.

When we got to Taiwan, we didn't know where exactly we were going or where we would be staying. Someone had given us the name of a pastor in Taiwan while we were still in Hawaii, but when I called the number we'd been given, someone answered who couldn't speak much English. I understood them to say that the person we were looking for was no longer pastoring, but I couldn't be sure of that because I didn't understand much.

A Foretaste of Glory Divine

One of our sisters was not feeling very well, so the other sister and I went for a long walk and prayed as we walked. In fact, we prayed and walked for the next seven hours. We didn't really know what to ask God, so we simply prayed in tongues. In this type of situation, I found that if I prayed in English I could pray negative things. If I was praying in the Holy Ghost, I could only pray that which was positive, that which was powerful, that which was the heart of God.

After seven hours of prayer, we went and called our contact number again, and this time the person who answered spoke English. I told them that God had sent us there, so he called the pastor of the church and told him, and he invited us to come to the church that night to share with his people and said they would like to take us out to eat afterward. This all sounded good to us, but especially the fact that they wanted to treat us to a meal. We had gone several days now without eating.

The one sister was now feeling so ill that she didn't want to go to church that night, but I insisted. "The place to be when you are sick," we had been taught, "is in church, not at home." So she got up, and got dressed, and we went down to meet the lady who was coming to take us to the church.

Lady Jane Lowder

When we saw the lady, we were very excited to realize that we already knew each other. I had met her in Israel, so we had a lot to talk about as we went on our way to the church.

They had told us that they would give each of us a few minutes to share our testimonies. When the time came, the older sister gave her testimony first, and she was completely healed the moment she stood up.

The other sister gave her testimony next, and then I gave a short one about how God had healed me, giving me brand new lungs. At the end of my testimony, the Lord gave me three wonderful words of knowledge, and I spoke them out. In each case, someone came forward, recognizing themselves as the person God was speaking about, He healed them, and they were slain in His presence. Then the pastor of the church came running, asking us to take the rest of the service and minister to his people as God led us.

I hadn't realized that this church was also a Bible school, so there were many students there who felt called by God and wanted to prepare themselves for His work. As I ministered, every single person in the place was slain in the Spirit, and about seventy-five percent of them were baptized in the Holy Spirit and spoke in other tongues. God had poured out His Spirit upon us.

After the service we went out and had something to eat. Later, after we had gotten back to our hotel, the pastor called me. It was about midnight. "I was so happy about what happened at the church tonight," he said, "and I'm wondering if you could stay for a few more days and minister to our people."

I said, "Let me ask the others."

I covered the receiver and told the other ladies that we had been asked to stay. Our problem was that we didn't have money to stay in the hotel, and we had been taught that we should not tell anyone about our needs, just take them to God. The pastor hadn't mentioned paying our hotel, so now we had a decision to make. Should we risk it? The other two answered that they were willing to do whatever I felt, so I told the pastor we would stay.

We had all been ready for bed, but now we got up and began praying. We wondered if we might need to spend the rest of the night in prayer. We didn't have money for three nights of hotel and meals, and the pastor hadn't made us any promises.

Often, in overseas ministry, there is no offering, as we are accustomed to give speakers in our Western countries. I had ministered many times when there was no offering at all, not even a few cents. We needed to depend on God. So there we were, praying up a storm, and suddenly the phone rang again. It was the pastor, and he said, "I'm sorry I forgot to say that we will take care of your hotel room, your food, and your transportation to any place you need to go while you're here." So we stayed and ministered for three more days.

On the final night of those three nights of meetings, someone prophesied that we should stay for seven more days. The pastor got up quickly and came over to us and said, "Are you willing to be obedient to what the Lord is saying?"

I said, "We are."

And so we stayed for the seven additional days. We actually ended up staying there for twenty-one days in that place, and during that time, we ministered in meetings all over town. Many of them were in Bible schools and seminaries, and we taught on the Holy Ghost and the outpouring of the Holy Ghost, and many received.

From there, God opened many doors around Taiwan, then the Philippines, Malaysia, Indonesia, and many other places (mostly among the Chinese people living there). The people we met in those days have remained good friends to this day.

A Foretaste of Glory Divine

And how God blessed us financially in that place! The offerings we received in Taiwan enabled us to go on to Hong Kong, China, the Philippines, India, Nepal, and many other places. We had been planning to go to Egypt, but we didn't get there on that particular trip.

We had started our trip with a little over seventy dollars each, and we had been away for about eight months, but with every step God had made a way where there was no way. We came back rejoicing in His goodness.

Most of the times, when I left for overseas, I expected to be gone for at least six months and often longer, and usually I had very little money with me when I left. Interestingly enough, when I came back, I always had more than I'd had when I left. God had blessed me along the way. When we go and bless others, God will be faithful to bless us.

Sometimes I did long fasts while I was traveling. At times, these were forced fasts, and at other times, it was because I chose not to eat so that I could pray and seek God. He makes a way for us where there is no way, when we activate our faith in His promises.

God's Presence Filled the Whole Place

ONE DAY I HAD A WONDERFUL experience in Taiwan. We'd had one service very early in the morning, then another service that started at nine and continued until around two. Then we went out to get something to eat. When we came back into the auditorium, there was a man praying at the altar.

He was on his face to the ground. (There was no carpet, just bare earth.) The presence of God was in that place so thick that I felt as if I would collapse. Instead of going to my room, where I had intended to pray again from four until six for the evening service, I thought "God, it is so wonderful that You have filled this place with Your Presence, with just this one man praying, I will stay right here."

God said to me, "I would fill the whole universe with just one person praying."

A Foretaste of Glory Divine

This was such an eye-opener for me, that when any person bows to God and cries out to Him, His presence permeates that place. No wonder, then, that when thousands gather together and sing praises unto the Lord, His presence comes. Where the Spirit of Lord is there is life, there is liberty, and there are miracles.

On that same trip to Taiwan, I was praying one day in the home of my hostess. At one time, she had been on fire for God, but then she and her husband had experienced some personal problems. One child was not well and did not do well in school. The family finances became strained, and her spirituality suffered.

I had asked her if she would come and pray with me each afternoon for the evening service. She came, but she was just sitting there, not praying. I encouraged her to speak in tongues, but she said that although she used to pray in tongues all the time, she couldn't do it anymore.

I said, "Of course you can. God never takes anything away from us. It is there even though you may not feel like it is."

She said, "For sure I don't feel like it is."

I continued to encourage her. "Please pray with me, even for just an hour. Lift up your voice with me now." Finally, she started praying in tongues, but she spoke for just a few minutes and stopped.

I took her hand and encouraged her not to stop. "Just speak it out loudly," I said, but she stopped again.

I was not discouraged. Again I took her hand and said, "Come on. You can do it." And she tried again. By the time the first hour was up, she was doing well, and we went on into the second hour.

By the time we had prayed two hours together, she was revived. She went on a forty-day fast, and God lifted her into a new place.

She was so excited that first day that she called her husband and asked him to try to make arrangements to come the next day. He came, and we had a great time praying together. The whole family was blessed because that sister pushed through her discouragement and sought God in the Spirit.

"Bariki! Bariki! Bariki!"

BEFORE I LEFT FOR KENYA one year I was praying in the camp tabernacle every night from about two until three in the morning. One night, as I walked across the front praying, I found myself saying, "Bariki, Bariki, Bariki" over and again. I said that word for days in prayer, although it didn't mean anything to me at the time.

When I got to Kenya, one day I was coming down the steps of a pastor's home, singing in other tongues, and he stopped me. He said, "Sister Jane, I know you don't know what you are saying. I know you don't know what you are singing, but you are singing in my language about the precious blood of Jesus that cleanses and makes one whole." Wow! That was wonderful!

We went to a service, and I was shouting out, "Bariki, Bariki," and he came up and asked if I knew what I was saying.

I said, "No, I'm speaking in other tongues."

He said, "You are saying, 'Bless you! Bless you! Bless you!'"

When I was in China one year, they asked me where I had learned Chinese. I was apparently speaking fluently as I was praying. They told me I was telling them to open their mouth and God would fill it.

I have been in other places where people were speaking in tongues, and they were speaking fluent English, although they spoke no English in the natural. How great is our God!

Just in Time

IN ONE MOUNTAINOUS AREA OF the Philippines, I visited a church and had the opportunity to speak over one of the local leaders. He was the Barangay Captain, but the people of the whole area honored him as their "datu." He got saved. Later that day, as he was going down the mountain in his vehicle, he was shot to death. When I learned of it, I was thankful that I'd had the privilege of bringing him into the Kingdom just in time.

Over the years, I prayed for thousands of people, and most of them were not famous, but some of them were.

One of these was Minister Salvador Laurel of the Philippines. I was invited to pray for him and his family in their home, and God gave me a wonderful word for him. Later, he was to become Vice President of that island nation. God had known it all along and had told him through me that He would raise him up as He had Moses.

Later, I had the opportunity again to visit and pray with him after he was sworn in and was about to leave to visit our country in his official capacity. When he got to the airport that day, customs inspectors found a gun in his suitcase, and a big political stink was made of it. He insisted that he hadn't put it there; it had been planted on him. Someone was not happy about his rise to power.

I prayed with Senator Emmanuel Pelaez who later became the Philippine ambassador to the United States.

I prayed for Don Enrique Locsin, for whom the barrio was named. I prayed for Teodoro Locsin, Sr, editor of the Philippine Free Press.

I prayed for the man who had served as executive secretary to President Ferdinand Marcos. His son was on drugs, and so he needed God's help.

I prayed for the colonel who was then head of Philippine intelligence. He was later promoted to general.

I spoke and ministered in Camp Crame and other military bases and prayed for many officers, as well as enlisted men. At Crame and a base in Iloilo, many men were born again, filled with the Spirit, and spoke in tongues. These were exciting opportunities to make an impact for God's Kingdom.

One of the Most Challenging Cases

ONE OF THE MOST CHALLENGING cases in my ministry overseas occurred in Singapore. I was speaking at a Bible study in a private home with thirty or forty people in attendance, and a young man was playing the guitar during the praise and worship. Each time I looked at him, I could see death all over him. No one had told me anything about him, but it seemed that he must have cancer. His hair had all fallen out, his skin was yellowish, and he was extremely thin. Still, there he was playing the guitar and worshipping the Lord.

That night I prayed for every single person in that place, and this young man was the last. When I came to him, God gave me a word to speak over his life. I prayed for God to give him strength, to pour out His Spirit upon him, and to bring life to him from the top of his head to the soles of his feet. Then I head myself saying these words, "And, yea, the Lord saith unto thee, 'I shall raise thee up, and thou shalt be one that shall go unto many places and preach and teach My Word. You shall be known as My son, and you shall be known as a man of faith.'"

As God went on and on, my brain clicked in, and I thought, "God, what is this? And where is it coming from?"

When I had finished prophesying over that young man, I would have loved to have pulled every one of those words back into my mouth. Everything about him looked like he was soon to die.

Afterward I heard his story. He had indeed been near to death, but the people of the church, his mother among them, took that word I had given him, made copies of it, and held on to it in prayer. They prayed day and night over the coming days, holding that word up to God, and the boy did the same.

His health did not recover quickly, and the family physician said that he probably only had weeks to live, so the family planned an around-the-world trip to give their son a chance to see as much of the world as possible before his death. His mother had not given up on him, however, and she took a copy of the prophecy with her on the trip and continued to hold it up to God in faith every single day.

A Foretaste of Glory Divine

The boy survived the trip, but when they had gotten back home, his health did not seem improved. In fact, he was weaker. He was now so weak that all chemotherapy treatments were suspended.

Then one morning, he said to his mother, "Mom, I want to go back and have another CAT scan."

The mother called the doctor and asked what he thought. The doctor said there was no reason to do more tests. The young man was in his last days, and they should just do anything possible to make him comfortable.

But this did not satisfy the young man. He got up the next morning and announced that he wanted to go and have the CAT scan. The mother called the doctor again, and the doctor said, "Well, it can't hurt anything. Whatever he wants, maybe you should let him do it, because he only has a few more days left." They went and had the CAT scan done, and it showed that there was not a trace of cancer in the young man's body. He had been completely set free and made whole.

He still didn't look like he was whole. He didn't have any hair, his skin was still yellowish, and he still had no strength, but he quickly began improving.

The next time I went to Singapore, I was invited to speak at a large Chinese gathering in a local coliseum. As I was walking down to the front of the place, a woman came running from the back and leaped at me. She came at me so forcefully that we both fell to the ground and went rolling. I thought, "My God, why is this woman attacking me like this?"

She was saying something, but the only thing I could understand was "heal." The woman couldn't speak English, and I surely didn't speak Chinese. I got up and straightened my hair, straightened my dress, and went and found my seat, but all the while my mind was pondering this strange event.

Later, when the pastor I was working with had arrived, I was able to ask him, "Who is that lady? And why was she jumping on me like that?" And I explained to him what had happened. He said we would be having lunch with her the very next day.

We went to the lunch, and there was all of her family sitting together around the table, and then her son came in, and we saw his transformation. He was completely healed, had gained his weight back, had all of his hair, and his color was wonderful. The last time I saw that young man he was serving as youth pastor for a church there in Singapore.

There is a river that flows within us, and if we will let it flow, amazing things will happen.

A Foretaste of Glory Divine

There may be times when we would like to take back our words, but if you know that they came from God, you can stand on them and keep on believing and see God bring something marvelous and wonderful to pass.

"He Is the One"

GOD WORKS INSIDE AND OUTSIDE of churches and crusade locations. He will work anywhere we happen to be at the moment.

Many years ago, I was visiting my sister in the hospital as she was giving birth to her little boy. In the same room with her was a young girl of about fourteen or fifteen who was also about to give birth. She was terrified and was crying a lot and, at first, nobody was there with her. Later her mother came, but instead of comforting her child, I couldn't believe what that mother did.

First of all, I couldn't believe that this girl had been left there to face this situation by herself. It was obvious that she was in extreme trauma. She was just a child herself, and yet here she was about to give birth to a child. It was undoubtedly a very difficult time in her life, and yet she had been there to face it all by herself.

Then, when the mother finally did come in, she went directly to the side of her daughter's bed, but instead of offering the words of comfort and encouragement the girl needed to hear in that moment, the mother began to berate her. She said, "Your daddy is going to come up here, and you are going to be in a *lot* of trouble because your daddy is *very* mad at you." And she went on to describe exactly what the daddy was going to do to his daughter.

Overhearing this, I couldn't help but think to myself, "What kind of person would do this to a child who is going through such a traumatic time of life, about to bring into the world a child that maybe she doesn't even want? Maybe she just got caught up in a bad situation, and emotion took over, but regardless of what happened, the fact was that a baby was coming, and yet the girl had been there to face the situation by herself, and now that the mother had come, instead of offering encouragement, she had nothing but threats to make.

Any mother can offer her child strength and encouragement, but this mother only made her child more miserable and more fearful of what was to come. It broke my heart, and I prayed, "Lord, what can I do at a time like this?"

I asked the mother if it would be okay for me to speak to her daughter. She said I could.

Lady Jane Lowder

I moved to the girl's side, took her hand, and asked her what her name was. She told me her name, and I said to her very gently, "I want to tell you something, and I want you to listen very closely. Jesus Christ, who gave His life for you, is standing right here with you tonight, and He is the One who formed that baby you have inside of you. He is the One who put joint to joint, bone to bone, and all that made up this marvelous creation. It took a lot for this child to get to this point, when you are about to give birth to it."

Occasionally, as I spoke, she would have another pain and cry out. Then I would continue. In between pains, I said to her, "Now the next time you have one of those pains, whisper the name of Jesus, and Jesus is going to help you. Jesus is going to strengthen you. Jesus is going to bring life and peace and joy to you."

I asked her if she had ever had an experience with Jesus, and she said she had gone to church when she was a little girl and had given her life to Him.

I asked if she remembered that day she had given her life to Jesus, and she said she did. I told her to go back to that day and pick it up again, because God was going to do something wonderful for her now. And He did.

Some time later, when I went to visit my sister in her home, she said to me, "That young girl you talked to in the hospital told me that if you ever came back to my house again to please bring you to see her."

We went to her house and ministered to her again, and she told me this: "When you stood by my bed and told me to call upon the name of Jesus, from that time on, peace came into me. All fear went out of my heart, and the extreme pain was gone."

God knows just what to speak in any given situation.

What Was More Important: Poland or My Own Mom?

I WAS IN POLAND WITH BROTHER Heflin and a team from the camp for meetings, and during that same time my mother was very sick back home. Every afternoon we gathered together and prayed for an hour or more before the night service, and Brother Heflin was believing that every afternoon we would have a fresh word from the Lord.

But sometimes, when life's trials come, our minds can become overtaxed, even as our spirits are alive and going to higher heights in the Lord. While the Lord is speaking great things into our spirits, our brain is going wild with all sorts of negative thoughts. That was what was happening to me this particular day.

I was having visions from the Lord, and, at the same time, I was being bombarded with thoughts of concern about my mom. The enemy was tormenting me, saying that my own mom wasn't healed while we were trying to bring healing to the people of Poland.

"How about her foot?" he tormented. "And what's happening with her that she doesn't talk anymore?" Here we were believing for miracles for the people who came to the services, for them to be saved and healed, to get out of wheelchairs and to be delivered from their afflictions, "But how about your mom?" I kept hearing.

The whole time God was giving me a prophetic word to speak to the people, a word that was life, a word that was powerful, a word that would be fulfilled that night in the ministry, my mind was filled with all sorts of thoughts and concerns about Mom. I was buffeted with those thoughts.

For some reason, Mom's foot had turned upward, and she could no longer walk. Worse, she had fallen into a stupor and stayed that way for the past two years. She was no longer able to communicate with any of us. We would say, "Momma, look at me," and she would look at us. But when we said anything else, she would just turn and look away. We could not seem to reach her. The enemy was now taking full advantage of this situation, and saying to me, "Where is God concerning your mother?"

Lady Jane Lowder

Sometimes our biggest battles, as servants of the Lord, come when we are moving to do something for Him, and the reality of our personal situations keep trying to intrude. I would be giving a prophetic word for the meeting that night, talking about signs, wonders, and miracles and, at that very moment, I would have a vision of my precious mother sitting in that wheelchair, unable to move her feet, unable to feed herself, and I heard the devil say, "What about your own mom?"

It was a tormenting thing, and I knew that if I was not careful that tormenting thing would take precedence, and I would be tempted to go with it.

"God spoke to me and said, "If your mom never walks again, your mom never talks again, and your mom never feeds herself again, I am still God, and I never fail." When He said that, all of the anxiety I was feeling for her disappeared.

God did great miracles there in Poland and also in Czechoslovakia. Many people were saved; many people were healed; blind eyes were opened; deaf ears were unstopped; great and wonderful things happened in those meetings, even though those tormenting thoughts were with me nearly every moment of every day. But I also want you to know that before that year had ended, Mom was up and out of her wheelchair. She was walking again, she began talking again, and she was able to feed herself again. Health officials had told us that she would never again do any of those things, but she was slowly returning to normal. God turned that situation around and gave Mom a new song to sing. He is a miracle-working God!

Persecution in Nepal

I WAS INVITED TO GO TO NEPAL and hold some outdoor meetings. It was a great honor.

When we went there in 1978 and 79 with a team of forty, there were only two churches in the Katmandu area. We split into four groups of ten and went out north, south, east, and west, preaching and distributing copies of God's Word.

We were not the only ones taking advantage of the crack in the door there. There were others who trekked through the mountains preaching the Gospel and distributing God's Word in the local language.

Today there are literally hundreds of churches around Nepal, but the only way to get to many of them is by walking. It can takes days to get from one village to another. It is a beautiful country, and it is a great privilege to be able to tell her people about Jesus.

Sometimes we had the opportunity to take the Gospel to a village for the first time or to places that had only one Christian. We had meetings there and saw many people come to the Lord.

Sometimes we went for just one person, and some didn't understand that. But Jesus died for each one of us individually. Just as He died for all of us, He died for each person. In one case, the person we were going for was the man mentioned in an earlier story.

This man suffered a lot for his faith. He was sometimes beaten to a pulp. His wife had been taken from him, and his children had to leave the village because their lives were in danger. The local people stole all of his goats, his sheep, and his fields. He and his brother had been taken outside the camp, beaten, and left for dead, but God had raised them up. He boldly went back into the village and put a sign on his door, *"As for Me and My House, We Will Serve the Lord."*

He was respected for having taken that stand and, after many years, God restored his land back to him. His goats were restored to him, and his children were allowed to come back home. His wife had been given to another man, so I'm not sure if she was ever able to come back to him. What a wonderful place that was to go and sow seeds of life and let our lights shine. Throughout the nations, God showed me *A Foretaste of Glory Divine!*

Part VI

Stories about Visions

My First Visions

WHEN I FIRST CAME TO KNOW THE Lord and began to have spiritual visions and dreams, I thought it was so wonderful just to hear His voice. He would show me things as I prayed. I didn't yet know anything about the glory realm or prophecy, the word of knowledge, or other giftings of the Spirit. Coming from a Methodist background, I had never heard about anyone having a vision, and yet the very day I received the Holy Ghost, at about eleven o'clock in the morning in my room, I saw a vision. It was so marvelous, so wonderful, and so glorious.

I saw the cross of Jesus, I saw Him on it, and I was drawn to that cross and heard the Lord speak to me from it. He said these words to me: "Now I have empowered you. Go and tell everything that I have called you to do. Tell everything that I have told you, and everything that I have done for you, go and tell." That was the moment that I began to speak in other tongues.

Lady Jane Lowder

I didn't have a clue about what I had. Not a clue! I had only heard one other person speak in tongues, and that was at a Full Gospel Businessmen's meeting.

Having had that wonderful vision of the Lord and having heard Him commissioning me to go and tell everything that He had done for me was just more than I could understand. The amazing thing was that I was delivered from the fear of standing before people, and I knew that, from that moment on, I had something to say, I had Somebody to talk about, and it wasn't myself. It was a man called Jesus. He was now my Friend, my Lover, and my Everything.

Everywhere I went, He went with me, and He was jealous over me. I knew that people had to be careful what they said about me, because they would have to deal with God. He was in love with me, and I was in love with Him. He was my God, and He was my Man.

He gave me another vision the next day, a Saturday morning. That same day I also discovered that we can speak in tongues anywhere and at anytime. I was told this by a Spirit-filled Methodist man who came into the restaurant. As soon as I could, I went into the rest room, got in one of the cubicles, and said to God, "Okay, Lord, if this is true, let it happen now." And it happened! I began to speak in other tongues again.

A Foretaste of Glory Divine

That night, I went home and got in my same wonderful spot, and I spoke in tongues. It was true. We could speak in tongues anywhere and at anytime.

I had never received any instruction on how to operate in the Holy Ghost. In fact, I had never heard anything good or bad about the Holy Ghost, or the baptism of the Holy Spirit, so I started out from zero.

That afternoon, about four o'clock, the Lord had given me a vision of a woman's face and told me that she had cancer. He said, "If you will go and pray for her, I will heal her." I knew the face because the woman came into the restaurant, and we attended the same church. But before the Lord touched me in 1975, I had begun going only on Christmas and Easter and other special days, so I hadn't known that the woman had cancer.

I called her and told her what God had said: If I would go and pray for her, He would heal her. She said, "Who told you that I had cancer?"

I said, "God did."

She said, "Well, you'd better come then." So I went.

She called her husband and her three children in from out in the yard, and I stood there in front of them all, not knowing what to do next. I didn't know how to pray. But here was this family standing expectantly in front of me, so I needed to do something.

They really didn't know what to do either. I guess they thought they probably needed to kneel to get me to pray for them, so they all got on their knees. I still just stood there, because I didn't know what to do or how to do it. Finally, the man looked up at me and said, "Well ... pray!"

I started praying, "Our Father, which art in Heaven, hallowed be thy name. Thy Kingdom come, thy will be done on earth as it is in Heaven." When I got to that place, there was no more English, and I began to speak in a language I didn't know. When this happened, my brain said, "You have messed it up now. You have really messed it up."

My brain was doing battle with my spirit, but I just kept on speaking in that heavenly language.

Then, suddenly, it stopped, just as quickly as it had begun. I still didn't know what to do. The only thing I could think of doing was getting out of there as quickly as possible.

I opened my eyes, and the man was crying, the woman was crying, and the three children were crying. I was the only one not crying, and I was scared to death. I thought, "I have really messed this thing up," so I left them all kneeling there on the floor. I went to my car, got in, and drove home as fast as I could go.

A Foretaste of Glory Divine

When I got home, I went into my room, fell on my face, and cried out to God. What had I done wrong?

Eleven days later this woman came back from the Duke Medical Center to say that she was completely healed of all traces of cancer.

That was the beginning of my learning to minister by seeing into the heavenlies, seeing what God was doing, and speaking out what He was showing me. I didn't know anything about the glory, anything about eternity, anything about the presence of God or the manifestations of the presence of God, but I was determined to learn.

Full of Acid

NOT LONG AFTER I HAD BEGUN serving the Lord, I was driving down the road one day on my way to Albemarle, North Carolina, and God gave me a picture, a vision. My eyes were wide open, but I saw a big red tomato. In fact, it was huge. I thought to myself, "What is this?"

Then, as I watched, a split formed in that big red tomato, and juice began to flow out of it. It was so real that if I had been an artist, I could have drawn a picture of it.

Next God asked me, "Do you know what the juice of a tomato will do to an aluminum pan?" I happened to know the answer to that question because I had bought a few aluminum pans, called tomato pans, for the restaurant where I worked. I'd had to buy a few of them because, if you put tomatoes in the same pan every day, the acid from the juice will eventually erode the surface and create a hole in it. So, occasionally, we had to go out and buy another tomato pan or be continually wiping up the tomato juice that leaked from the holes.

Because I knew that, I answered, "It will make a hole in it."

The Lord simply said to me, "You are going to meet someone like that tomato; they are full of acid." The vision went away, and I didn't think anymore about it.

I decided to stop by the place where I had worked, to get an ice cream cone and say hello to the people I knew, and then I would be on my way.

While I was in the restaurant, a woman I knew came in. Seeing me there, she tapped me on the shoulder and said to me, "I would like to speak to you for a moment."

I said, "Okay, let me go pay for my ice cream, and then I'll come back and talk with you."

As I was paying for my ice cream, that great big red tomato came before my eyes again, and God said, "This is she."

I went over to talk with the lady. She was someone I had gone to church with most of my young life, and that day she wanted to lash out against those who speak in tongues. She was very bitter because her daughter had received the baptism of the Holy Spirit at a Full Gospel Business Men's meeting, and her life had been dramatically changed. God had already showed me this through the vision before she even began her tirade. He is so faithful. He not only showed me what I was about to face but He also prepared me for it and showed me how to deal with it.

A Golden Shovel

I HAVE ALWAYS HAD MORE VISIONS while I was working than when I was on my face in prayer. One day three of us, two men and myself, were working backfilling the basement of the camp snack bar. The men left and never came back, and I was the only one left out there with that shovel. I asked the Lord, "Why is this? Why am I still out here, and nobody else is here?" In reply, He gave me a wonderful vision.

In the vision, God showed me a golden shovel, and in that shovel was something like sand and dirt. He said to me, "Every grain of this represents souls." This gave me a new kind of energy, so that the shovel became light, the work effortless, and I worked on and on, filling up that ditch.

I have found that you can tap into a place in God when you are tired, and He will energize you to the point that you don't feel tired any longer, and you can keep on working endlessly and accomplish whatever needs to be accomplished.

A Blank Slate

ONE OF THE THINGS I LEARNED to ask God to do early on was to make my mind just like a blackboard that has been erased. I especially asked Him to do this when I was ministering to someone. If I knew a person, I could think many things about them. But even if I had heard something about them, what assurance did I have that what I had heard was true? If I had a blank mind and was not thinking my own thoughts, then I could see in the Spirit what God wanted to say, what came forth from my lips would be from Him, and I would minister life, strength, joy, and peace to those round about me.

An Arm of Light

EACH MORNING WE PRAYED together from eight to nine, and one day, as I was praying, I saw a vision. God showed me an arm of light. It was pure light, and it was right there next to me, and I knew that the Lord was showing me His arm. It was outstretched, and I could see that His hand was open.

I was thrilled that day to realize that in a few second's time God could show me something so marvelous and so wonderful for that specific moment. If we could only open to Him, He would allow us to draw from His wonderful Spirit and would show us things that we needed to know right then.

I was still a very young Christian and didn't know many scriptures or many church doctrines when God began to show me things in the Spirit. These were things that pertained to the ministry, but also to daily life, and to other people. At the time, I didn't have a lot of scripture to back up such a thought, but I knew what I was experiencing was God, and so I pondered over it and I began to look up scriptures that confirmed it.

It didn't take me long to learn that visions come from God and that He can show us what we need in the moment for our ministry. Consequently, God spoke to me and taught me many wonderful things by seeing in the Spirit.

One of the wonderful things I saw in the Spirit in my very early times of walking with the Lord was a tiny lamb. It was a real four-legged lamb, and I heard the Lord speak to me, as I looked at that lamb. He said, "It's the blood of the Lamb that sets men free."

Then my vision began to flash like a neon light from that little four-legged lamb to Jesus on Calvary, and, through this, God began to teach me about Jesus becoming the Lamb that gave His life for us. Even though I had known this in a sense from the times I had gone to church as a child, He now focused light on it and made it very real to my spirit. Jesus is the Lamb, and it is the power of His blood that will set men free, keep them free, protect them, and carry them forward.

God also began to give me words of knowledge in vision, and this proved to be very effective in my ministry overseas. I prayed for thousands of people in this way.

"I Am Healing You"

IN MY FIRST MEETINGS IN Alexandria, Egypt, I saw a vision of a man falling from a ladder. I saw him landing on his shoulder, and saw that it had happened seven years before. I spoke out that there was someone there who had fallen from a ladder seven years before and, since then, hadn't been able to use his arm in the same measure. I declared, "God says, 'I am healing you.'"

But nobody said anything. Nobody claimed it, so the enemy quickly came to sow a seed of doubt in my mind and to tell me that I had missed God. My brain was saying, "You have really missed it. There is nobody here like that. Nobody is claiming it. You're just imagining things."

While these thoughts were going through my head, God gave me another vision, this one of a lady with a crook in her back, and he showed me where she was sitting in the back. God healed her.

Lady Jane Lowder

On Sunday night, a man came to me and said, "I'm that man who fell from the ladder seven years ago. When I came to this church, I did not come as a believer. I came to hinder the meeting, but when you called out that word, God healed me and set me free." During the course of that week he had gotten saved and filled with the Holy Ghost. What wonderful things God was doing!

Imprisoned for His Faith

AT ONE POINT, ONE OF OUR Nepali brothers was imprisoned for his faith. He had been a friend of the camp for many years, since Sister Ruth Heflin had visited Nepal in the 1960s, and he had been instrumental in making all of the arrangements for the teams that spread out throughout the Himalayas, taking the Gospel wherever they found an open door. This changed the course of his country. Now I was praying for him a lot.

Mary Wagner and I were traveling in ministry through Hong Kong and China and then Kenya, and all through this trip, I had a reoccurring vision of the mouth of a huge snake. The mouth was open, as if ready to strike, and I could see down the snake's throat. I could also see the roof of his mouth, his teeth, and his beady eyes. I had that same vision over and over again.

I didn't know for sure if God was telling us that *we* were in danger, but I knew that seeing a snake didn't mean something good, so every time I had the vision I would tell Mary about it. It kept coming back, but I still didn't understand it. Snakes do bite, and their bite can be venomous, so maybe we were in some sort of danger, we reasoned.

Then, while we were in Kenya, somebody on the bus with us had a vision of the two of us going to Nepal (where our brother was still in prison). We decided we needed to go there, but we felt that we could not call ahead and announce our coming (because we had been warned not to say anything about the Lord on the phone or to ask any questions about our brother's imprisonment, the length of his sentence, etc.)

We flew into Kathmandu and went to the house where he and his family lived, but nobody was home except the dog. We just hung around there until someone came. When his wife knew that we intended to try to see him in the prison the next day, she cautioned us. The prison officials probably would not allow it.

That night I had another vision. I saw that same snake head again, but I saw something new this time. I saw a hand holding the snake's throat from behind, and I understood that the mouth was gaping open like I had seen it because of the hand that was gripping it. The snake could not close its mouth.

The Lord said, "The vision is for your Nepali brother. Tell him that not many days from now he will be out, and that the enemy will no longer be able to strike at him."

I told his wife the vision and what God had said, but she responded, "Oh, he's going to be there for six years. They have already told him that. He's already been tried and convicted, and sentenced to six years."

I didn't quite know how to respond. "Well, God says he is going to be out within a few days," I said.

The wife was still unsure if I would be able to see my brother or not. She said there were also some English-speaking people in jail there (Australians). "If they don't allow you to see my husband, we will call for those foreigners to come, and you can talk to them instead. Either way, you will have to stand at a distance to speak."

We went and were allowed to visit our brother. As the wife had said, however, we had to stand back a distance while we spoke. It was an amazing scene. All of the visitors were speaking at the same time, and everyone had to somehow hear the voice they were intended to hear.

Lady Jane Lowder

When I saw my brother, a big lump rose up in my throat, and for a minute I couldn't say anything, and neither could he.

Then he managed to say, "Hello."

I said, "Hello," in return, and we talked a little, but we had to keep our conversation to generalities.

The next day I was able to go again, and this time our visit was much more productive. They brought our brother outside and allowed him to sit on a little stool. I was able to tell him the vision God had given me about the snake and about the hand and what God had said it all meant.

He was on a forty-day fast, and someone served us hot tea. It was the last time I was allowed to get that close to him.

We could only be in Nepal for five days, but on our way to the airport, we went by the jail again, and I was able to see our brother one more time. I felt that it was a critical visit, but what could I say that would encourage him? I asked the Lord, "Please give me something that will encourage him, some word that would lift his spirits." I was expecting God to tell me something wonderful, something that would turn my brother's world upside down. I was surprised now by what the Lord said.

A Foretaste of Glory Divine

The year we had been up in the mountains and our sister had broken her leg, the night before that a man of the village where we were staying had gotten drunk, becoming very angry, and starting to argue with our guide. God told me to speak to the man and that He would put words in my mouth. I thought surely He was going to give me something very wonderful.

I went to the man and asked him if I could speak to him, not having a clue about what I was going to actually say. He gave me permission to speak, and then all I had to say was: "It is getting very late, and we need to go. If you don't mind, we would like to sleep now because we have to walk very early in the morning."

These simple words took away all the man's anger, and we went on our way in peace. It was a word of wisdom from the Lord.

Now, as we stood in front of the jail talking to our brother, God gave me a word for him. He said, "Ask him if he remembers the lowly Man of Galilee."

I said, "Brother, do you remember the lowly Man of Galilee?"

He said, "Oh, yes, I remember Him."

I said, "He says to tell you that not many days from now, you will be out of this place."

I was standing there thinking, "God, You are so wonderful. Only a Christian would know that Jesus was 'the lowly Man of Galilee.' "

As I was standing there thinking about this, God told me to ask my brother if he remembered Brother Jude. I did this. He smiled and responded, "Yes, I do remember Brother Jude."

I said, "He says to tell you to keep on praying in the Holy Ghost, building up your most holy faith."

Mary and I flew from there to India, where we got on the wrong plane, went to the wrong place, and missed the first night of our scheduled meetings.

By the time we got home, several months later, the news had arrived that our Nepali brother was out of jail. There had been a sudden turnaround in that nation's policy toward Christians. Believers would now be permitted to speak of their faith.

God has a way of saying what He wants to say. He has given us the tongue of the learned that we might speak a word in due season to those who are in need. In this case, it came through a wonderful vision.

Visions for Those I Prayed for

THROUGH THE YEARS, GOD has also given visions to many of the people I've prayed for. For instance, I prayed for a mentally challenged boy of eight or ten, and he was taken to Heaven to meet the Lord Himself.

He was saved in a morning meeting, received the Holy Ghost that night and then had the vision. He saw himself climbing a ladder, and when he got up to the top, Jesus was there waiting for him. He called the boy by name and said to him, "Welcome to My world!"

He then walked with Jesus down the streets of Heaven and later described the river of life, the throneroom of God and what it was like to personally meet Abraham.

God did such a marvelous thing in that young man's life that he went back to school talking about Jesus. Impressed, his teachers gathered a crowd of people together and invited parents and other teachers to come and hear his vision. God used him to bring a lot of healings, salvations, and other good things.

He may never have spoken in public before, but when you have seen Heaven, when you have seen Jesus, and when you have heard His voice, everything changes, everything turns to something marvelous and wonderful, and God will do it for you too.

"All Your Need"

WE ARE ALL FAMILIAR WITH the passage that promises:

> *But my God shall supply all your need according to his riches in glory by Christ Jesus.*
> Philippians 4:19

A very different revelation of this passage came alive for me when I was invited to preach in a certain church. One of the first things the pastor said to me when I got there was, "I want you to be sure and pray for my brother while you're here. He lives just across the street."

I said, "Tell him to come to the meetings, and I'll be happy to pray for him."

We were in that place for four days, and every day the pastor reminded me that he wanted me to be sure to pray for his brother, and I answered him the same way every time: "If he comes to the meetings,

I'll pray for him." But as we finished up the last night of the meetings, the brother still hadn't shown up.

God did so many wonderful things that night that we didn't get back to the pastor's house until about one o'clock in the morning. As we were pulling up at the house, he said, "Oh, my brother's here." And when he said that, something rose up in me.

I thought, "Well now, he couldn't come to the meeting any one of the four nights we were there, but now he shows up at one o'clock in the morning and wants me to pray for him."

Why did that bother me so much? Well, sometimes, when people ask us to pray for them, they're not asking us to say a simple, "God bless them, help them, and strengthen them." They are believing that God will use us to give them a word that will provide guidance and answers for their life situations. And that night I was just pressed out of my seams, pressed beyond my realities, mainly because of the thoughts I was having. If this man really needed God and wanted God, why hadn't he come to the church services? I didn't voice it, but I sure was thinking it.

But that was a wrong attitude. God didn't tell us to choose whom we will pray for. If people are around us, they are there to be prayed for, and we can't make our own judgments about what they might or might not need. In the end, I agreed to go across the street to the brother's house.

The man was there with his wife, and I didn't have a clue about what God wanted to do for them. I had never met them before and didn't know anything about them.

I said to them, "Let's join hands and sing to the Lord." I was delaying because I didn't know what else to do. I needed to hear from God because I didn't have a thing for them.

We joined hands and began to sing a song to the Lord. It was a good way to get the answer. God understands what we need, and He understands what the people around us need.

As we were singing, I had a vision of the man and saw him preaching in a foreign country. The Lord said, "Tell him he is going to return to that country to preach."

As we continued praising the Lord, I went over and took the man's hands and began to share with him the vision God had given me.

I said, "I see you in a certain country preaching, and I see you leaving that country. God says to tell you that you will go back there."

After I had said that, I received more and continued, "God said to tell you, 'I am reconnecting you and putting you back together, and I will bring you forth into that place I have already promised you, and that which was separated and that which was taken away, this night I am mending it."

By this time, the man was on his face on the floor weeping loudly before the Lord. His wife was sitting nearby, but she, too, was weeping, although more quietly.

Even though I didn't have a clue about what was happening, I said to the brother, "God wants you to renew your walk with Him because He has not cast you aside."

He wept and wept and cried unto God, and while he was weeping, God gave me a vision for the woman he had introduced as his wife. I saw her mending an afghan. It had a big hole in it where it had been torn, and she was trying to put it back together, but the work was very uneven. God said to me, "Tell her that the hole that's been ripped, I'm putting it back together, and you will never know that it has been ripped." When I said that, she, too, hit the floor, weeping and crying out to God.

Afterward they were hugging each other, but as I turned to head back to the house where I was staying, I still didn't have a clue about what God had done.

A Foretaste of Glory Divine

The pastor decided to go with me, and as we got to his front door, he said to me, "You don't know what God just did, do you?"

I said, "No I sure don't."

He said, "My brother was in the country you mentioned preaching, and while he was gone, his wife ran off with another man. When he came home, he was devastated.

"He was able to pick himself up and continue preaching and teaching for several years, even though they remained separated. Then one night, as he was on his way to a revival meeting he was holding, he saw his wife in a car in front of him with the other man. He never went to church that night. Instead, he followed them, and after that he has never gone back to church.

"He has never preached again since that night, even though God restored their marriage, physically that is. The hole you saw was pertaining to the marriage, and God said, 'I'm going to put it back together and I'm going to mend it so that you will not know that it was ever ripped.' " How wonderful God is!

I had the opportunity to go back to that church about six months later, and the brother and his wife were in the meetings. They had done their vows over, and they were doing very well.

Lady Jane Lowder

On that first trip, the next day after praying for them, I was driving down the interstate on my way to visit my mother, and it suddenly hit me that when God said that He would supply our every need, He had a lot more than money in mind. He meant our need for everything, our need, whatever it happens to be at the moment. He will supply our need for every vision. He will supply our need for every word, for everything that we pray for, for whatever the particular person standing before us is needing. God is the One who supplies.

I got so happy that I had to stop my car, get out, and dance around a little, speaking in tongues.

Cars slowed, and people looked warily at me. One man asked, "Are you all right?"

"Yes," I said, "I'm all right. I'm just happy."

He said, "I believe you are."

I couldn't help myself. I was so excited that God would supply all of my need according to His riches in glory, not only my personal need, but also what I needed to offer to others as well.

Healing in Shops and Stores

I HAVE BEEN IN PLACES IN the Philippines, Nepal, India and other countries, and when I walked into a local shop of some sort, God began showing me something about someone who was there. It was not a church, and no one was worshipping, but God saw a need and sent me to meet it.

With one lady in the Philippines, God showed me that she had terrible pain in her back. I had just gone in her store to buy a Pepsi-Cola, but when she waited on me, God gave me a vision of her suffering.

I said to her, "You have pain in your back, and Jesus wants to heal you."

She started crying and said, "Yes."

She came out from behind the counter, and I prayed for her. She fell to the floor, and when she got up, all her pain was gone.

Lady Jane Lowder

She locked the door of her shop, and within about fifteen minutes she had gathered some seventy-five people under the trees because she wanted them to also meet this wonderful Jesus and be touched and healed by Him. Isn't our God wonderful!

It even happened right here in America. One Sunday, after I had ministered, a pastor took us to lunch. As I was eating God spoke to me about the dishwasher and said to me, "I want you to go and pray for her."

I asked someone if I could go and see the dish room, explaining that I formerly worked in a restaurant and would like to go back and see their operation. They welcomed me to go back, and, sure enough, a woman was back there working.

I said to her, "While I was eating, God spoke to me and told me to come back here and to tell you that your daughter is going to be all right." With that, she began to weep. Her daughter had been operated on that very morning. She fell on her knees right there in the restaurant and wept at the goodness of Jesus.

"Build Up Yourself"

ONE DAY I SAW IN A VISION AS if a cloud had been rolled out to form a banner, and on that banner were these words, "BUILD UP YOURSELF."

I thought about that all day long, and as I prayed about it, the Lord showed me another kind of a banner. This one said, "MOST HOLY FAITH."

I thought about that one for a while. Then, on the third day came the key: "SPEAKING IN TONGUES." God said to me, "I am going to renew and revive the Spirit, the gifting of speaking in other tongues, for it is the key for My people to build their faith in Me."

How wonderful! Visions are so powerful!

The Restoration of Broken Lamps

ON ONE OCCASION, WHEN another camp sister and I were ministering in Taiwan, we were praying every day, seeking God for the needs of the people. Sometimes, while we were praying, I would start laughing; other times, I would start crying. And sometimes you could hardly tell the difference between the laughing and the crying. God began to show me that in the laughter there is a travail, and there is a travail in the weeping as well.

I don't mean that prayer should always be a sad occasion, but there is something that comes to you in a moment's time which causes you to cry out from the innermost part of your being, for that moment, for that time, for that people, and for that which God is showing you. Sometimes it seems to be laughable, but those things we would call laughable, if we would look at them carefully, we would no longer

A Foretaste of Glory Divine

think of them as so laughable. This is what was happening as I was praying.

One afternoon, as I was praying, God took me out of my spirit, and I saw a great valley. In this valley there were many lamps. I don't know if you would call it a graveyard of lamps, or maybe it would be more like a junkyard, more or less, of lamps. It was a valley that was full of broken lamps, or lanterns, with all kinds of things wrong with them. They had been discarded and rejected, and they had no light in them, but you could still look at every one of them and see that it was a lamp, it was a lantern, or it had given forth light at one time.

As I looked at this scene, I began to weep, and my mind was carried away to Ezekiel and his valley of dry bones. I know that the valley in question spoke of Israel, but anybody who has any knowledge of the Word of God knows that lamps refer to the members of the Body of Christ, those who have been washed in the blood of Jesus, those who have, at some time, shone forth in darkness.

As I looked upon those lamps, I began to weep because they had been rejected, and as I continued to look at them, suddenly the Lord appeared on a hill of that valley. I can't describe the depth of the valley or the vast number of broken, discarded and rejected lamps that were there, no light shining out of them. On some of them, the globe was broken. Some of them had critical pieces missing. On others, the handle was broken off. All of them had been discarded for good reason. But now here was Jesus appearing over the top of the valley, and as I saw Him there, He said to me, "Bring them all to Me." At the moment when He said, "Bring them all to Me," the weeping ceased and laughter took hold of my innermost being. In that moment, I could see the greatness of God in the power of His life, in the power of His love, in the power of His desire for these lamps which were no longer burning.

He said, "Bring them all to Me, and I will restore them. I will refurbish them and cause them to shine again. I will cause them to arise and to go forth throughout the nations of the earth and bring forth light, even unto the dark places." What could be more wonderful? Vision enriches our lives and brings us *A Foretaste of Glory Divine.*

Part VII

Stories about My Mom and Dad

"Where Was God?"

IT WAS A LONG TIME INTO MY Christian walk before I began to think deeply about certain things that had happened in my life before I came to know God. Some of the things that happened as a result of Dad having his stroke and not being able to work anymore deeply affected our whole family. Things happened between each of us and Dad because his condition left him frustrated and angry.

One day God suddenly showed me something in the Spirit. It just came to me very quickly and quietly. I had a quick vision of something that had happened in my home when I was a little girl, something that I had always questioned God about. It had to do with Mom being hurt. God spoke to me that day and said, "I was there all the time." In that moment, I had a sudden knowing and understanding. Yes, He was there. If He had not been there, she might not have survived, and our lives would have been a disaster.

Lady Jane Lowder

Why did He say it? Looking back on those days, I realized that I had wondered where God was at that moment. Why hadn't He intervened?

Now, forty years later, I had my answer. He had been there the whole time.

Then God made it very personal for me. He said, "Not only was I there all the time, but I was with *you* all the time." Wow! That said it all.

A Tribute to My Father

I MUST PAY TRIBUTE TO MY FATHER. Where we lived as children was way out in the country, so far out that I often said we had to pipe in the sunshine. Our nearest neighbors were a long way away. Further up the road were a few more primitive houses surrounded by woods. Today, you would never know this because modern houses stand in what was once our wilderness pasture field.

We were poor, but I thank God my dad didn't sit down and say, "The well dried up, so we might as well sit down and dry up with it." He could have, and we could have sat out there and dried up. But he didn't dry up, and he didn't let us dry up. He made us go along with whatever was going along at the moment.

Dad was tough, and he demanded a lot of us. There was always a lot of work to be done around our place and never much time for play. Even on rainy days, we shelled corn or cleaned up the barn, forking out all the manure. Our rainy days were just as busy as any other day of the week.

We planted twenty or thirty acres of corn, and then, when the harvest was in, we shelled the seed corn by hand, cob by cob. That took a lot of time.

In reality, back in those days (the 1940s and 50s), there were not many fun places to go or fun things to do, like there are for children today. As farm children, we did feel resentment at times for not having the things city people had, but there were many things we did have. We always had country ham on our table, for instance, and we had lots of potatoes and beans. We had fresh eggs every day and fresh butter and our own home-baked bread.

We might have had holes in our shoes and patches on our clothes, but we sure ate well (we raised it all ourselves). In one way, we were poor, but in another way, we were actually rich.

But children don't always appreciate what they have until later in life. Today, I'm afraid, we spoil our children, giving them too much and expecting too little of them.

Children need chores to do so that they can learn responsibility. They need to be made aware that life is not just a game. The children of today sometimes grow up not knowing how to do anything much at all. When they have a need, all they know to do is go to Dad and Mom. But what will happen when Mom and Dad are no longer there to respond to those needs? Each of us needs to learn to stand on our own feet and fend for ourselves.

As children, we were protected, never allowed to go out at night or to go home with neighbor children and spend the night with them and do whatever they were doing. Dad was very protective in this way. I didn't appreciate it all at the time, but I surely do now.

Dad didn't teach us a lot about the Bible, but he did take us to church every Sunday, and we were known in the community as Christians. We didn't do what were considered bad things. For instance, we didn't go to dances (unless it was a square dance that was a family affair, and then Dad went with us), and we were not allowed to do many of the other things other children did. Dad kept us under those wonderful reins and showed us a more excellent way.

In our home, we honored God, and we honored our Dad. He made the decisions, not his children. He made good decisions, and he taught us to make good decisions. To me, his advice on giving a good day's work for a good day's pay proved invaluable and was the reason I was always promoted. Dad taught us how to live honorably, and instilled in us the wisdom to know that our good name and our word meant everything and that we should never say we would do something and then not follow through on it. "If you say it, then you do it," we were taught.

Dad was our example in this regard. If he said something to us, we knew that he meant it, and he would never take it back. And when he corrected us, he corrected us, and that was that. We knew we had been corrected. He made sure we never forgot it.

Dad was not perfect, and there were aspects of his character that we came to resent and other aspects that it took us years to learn to appreciate.

Many of us tend to look at Father God in the same light as we do our earthly fathers, but God is so much greater than our earthly fathers that there is little room for comparison. Earthly fathers fail, but God never does.

Having had years to ponder these truths, I have to say that, as tough as he was, my earthly father was a wonderful one in so many ways. He was good to me, and he showed me a lot of wonderful things that prepared me for life.

A Foretaste of Glory Divine

There was one specific way I always wished Dad could have been different. He was not demonstrative when it came to declaring his love for us. He didn't often tell us that he loved us. He did always say, as he was spanking us, "If I didn't love you, I wouldn't be doing this." But children don't often understand that sort of reasoning. If that was love, maybe it was better not to be loved. I took this attitude and personally began to close off love.

I was fortunate in that I met God, my real Father, the One who *is* love, the One who loves us unreservedly and keeps on loving us regardless. With this Father, when I fell, He didn't respond with a leather strap. Instead, He picked me up and assured me that I could make it. This Father never put curse words on me. Instead, He assured me that I was wonderful and lovely, and I was lovely because He was lovely.

This Father believed in me, and I found Him to be so wonderful that I could go to Him with anything at all, pour my heart out to Him, and He would never rebuke me or send me away. Instead, He took me in, held me tight to Himself, and showed me a better way.

Right or not, I had allowed my earthly father's actions to wound me, but God opened to me His fountain of love and, with it, forgiveness. He forgave me, and I found myself forgiving my father. Just one touch of God's love removed a lifetime of resentment and disappointment that had built up toward Daddy.

Having a stroke at such a young age was not his choice. He couldn't help it that he lost the mobility that had enabled him to work so hard. Before that stroke, he had been working two jobs to support us. He worked in the cotton mill and still kept the farm running.

It would be difficult for any of us with sound bodies to imagine the frustration Dad felt at losing the full use of his arms and his ability to speak clearly and normally. Most of all, he was frustrated by his inability to work and provide for his family. How would we have reacted under those circumstances? We might never know for sure. In time I came to realize this more fully.

Most importantly, I can now say that I know that Daddy loved me. He never once put his arms around me and told me in so many words that he loved me, but I know that he did because God told me he did. Daddy's problem was just that he couldn't express the love he felt. But Daddy was a treasure, and I pay tribute to him today.

A Tribute to My Mother

LIKEWISE IT TOOK ME MANY YEARS to realize how great and wonderful a mother I'd had and what a spiritual strength she had been to me. Even when she was sick in bed, unable to get up and unable to take care of herself, I would still hear her singing to the Lord in the night. Mom always sang.

How could I ever forget hearing her singing as she worked in the fields? How could I ever forget the words that meant so much to her:

> 1. *Tempted and tried, we're oft made to wonder*
> *Why it should be thus all the day long;*
> *While there are others living about us,*
> *Never molested, though in the wrong.*

Refrain:
Farther along we'll know more about it,
Farther along we'll understand why;
Cheer up, my brother, live in the sunshine,
We'll understand it all by and by.

Lady Jane Lowder

2. *Sometimes I wonder why I must suffer,*
Go in the rain, the cold, and the snow,
When there are many living in comfort,
Giving no heed to all I can do.
   (Refrain)

3. *Tempted and tried, how often we question*
Why we must suffer year after year,
Being accused by those of our loved ones,
E'en though we've walked in God's holy fear.
   (Refrain)

4. *Often when death has taken our loved ones,*
Leaving our home so lone and so drear,
Then do we wonder why others prosper,
Living so wicked year after year.
   (Refrain)

5. *"Faithful till death," saith our loving Master;*
Short is our time to labor and wait;
Then will our toiling seem to be nothing,
When we shall pass the heavenly gate.
   (Refrain)

6. *Soon we will see our dear, loving Savior,*
Hear the last trumpet sound through the sky;

A Foretaste of Glory Divine

Then we will meet those gone on before us,
Then we shall know and understand why.
　(Refrain)

1. *There's a land that is fairer than day,*
And by faith we can see it afar;
For the Father waits over the way
To prepare us a dwelling place there.

Chorus:
　In the sweet by and by,
　We shall meet on that beautiful shore;
　In the sweet by and by,
　We shall meet on that beautiful shore.

2. *We shall sing on that beautiful shore*
The melodious songs of the blessed;
And our spirits shall sorrow no more,
Not a sigh for the blessing of rest.

3. *To our bountiful Father above,*
We will offer our tribute of praise
For the glorious gift of His love
And the blessings that hallow our days.

　　Mom loved to sing *Will the Circle Be Unbroken,* and she loved that wonderful chorus to *Blessed Assurance:*

Lady Jane Lowder

This is my story, this is my song,
Praising my Savior all the day long.
This is my story, this is my song,
Praising my Savior all the day long.

And that was Momma's legacy to us.

When Daddy had his stroke, and life seemed finished for him (as far as being able to work and provide for the family), instead of becoming despondent, Mom rose up. She never expressed fear, and I never heard her complain. She never once said that we couldn't or we weren't going to make it. Instead, I heard her singing to the Lord and then telling us it was time to go to the field. She was always working to bring about those wonderful things that were needed.

Mom had no formal education, and she couldn't read, but she had a wonderful relationship with the Lord and a faith in Him that, even in the midst of the greatest obstacles, we could go on, and we could achieve the goals that were before us.

Back in those days, our goals were very simple: surviving from one year to the next, just going on with life. But we made it somehow, and Momma went on to live a rich, full life. God was good to her, and I am blessed today to have had her as my mother.

A Foretaste of Glory Divine

Mom's mother had also been a Christian, and Mom missed her. That's why her favorite song was always "If I Could Hear My Mother Pray Again." It went something like this:

1. How sweet and happy seem those days of which I dream,
When memory recalls them now and then!
And with what rapture sweet my weary heart would beat,
If I could hear my mother pray again.

Chorus:
If I could hear my mother pray again,
If I could hear her tender voice as then!
So glad I'd be, 'twould mean so much to me,
If I could hear my mother pray again.

2. She used to pray that I on Jesus would rely,
And always walk the shining gospel way;
So trusting still His love, I seek that home above,
Where I shall meet my mother some glad day.

3. Within the old home-place her patient, smiling face

Lady Jane Lowder

Was always spreading comfort, hope and cheer;
And when she used to sing to her eternal King,
It was the songs the angels loved to hear.

4. Her work on earth is done, the life-crown has been won,
And she will be at rest with Him above;
And some glad morning she, I know, will welcome me
To that eternal home of peace and love.

She especially loved to sing that second verse and the chorus.

You are blessed today if you still have your mother with you. Learn to appreciate her while you have time.

After Daddy had his stroke and we all felt that he was not very fair with us, if we would try to approach Mom about it, she would hush us up immediately. "No!" she insisted, "you cannot say that about your dad. He *is* your dad, and he is sick." She simply never allowed us to say bad things about him. She remained faithful to him in every way.

Sometimes I marveled at this because there were things that went on in our house that were not very pleasant, but Mom never once took our side on any of this. Whenever we went to talk to her about any of these issues, we were forced to adjust our thinking to hers. There was no compromise when it came to this subject.

Mom worked as hard as any man and never complained about what had to be done, and God only knows that it was work: morning, noon, and night (and, sometimes, way into the night). After J.C. turned sixteen and started driving the school but, we had to get up at three fifteen or three thirty to begin our daily chores and get done in time to leave with the bus, but Mom would always be up before us. J.C. and I were always second, so that we could build a fire.

While Mom was making breakfast, we went to the pasture to get the cows in, feed them, put out the hay. Only then did we come back to the house to have one of her hot country breakfasts. Then she would go with us back to the barn to milk those cows (until we eventually lost them too).

At first, it was just the three of us — Mom, J.C., and myself, but as the others got older, they also joined us in the milking. This all had to be done before we left for school.

We had to leave home by six thirty or seven to catch the bus for school, and then we came back in the afternoon at four and started the routine all over again.

Lady Jane Lowder

Mom was always there when we got home. She might be out in the field working, but we always knew that there would be a treat waiting for us. We could just go to the oven and open it, and there we would find Mother's love inside in the form of a fresh apple pie. We would get that apple pie out, pour some wonderful fresh milk over it, and enjoy it. That was Mother's love in action!

We also found her love in the refrigerator! In fact, we found Mother's love everywhere we went. Did we always honor her love? No, as children we didn't always honor it. We didn't even recognize that it *was* Mother's love. We ate what she prepared and were thankful that it tasted good, but we didn't often give thanks to the source of it all. As with most of us, down through the years we were often guilty of not recognizing our mother's sacrifices and being thankful for them. But those were wonderful years, and she gave us so much. Her mother's love was everywhere.

When it came time to put our school clothes on or our church clothes, we would find that Mother's love had pressed them and made the collars stiff with corn starch and water (which was our starch back then). On Sunday morning, we had crisp dresses that Mother's love had hung neatly in the closet. Those dresses might have some age to them, and they had not been elegant to start with, but Mother's love had brought forth the beauty in them.

Mother's love! You can find it everywhere in the house, if you just look for it.

One of the reasons we never had to fear the coming of winter was that Mom had worked so hard and helped us work so hard to be ready for it. All summer long, she had been canning and storing those jars in the cupboard. We always canned a hundred and fifty quarts of green beans, and we ate so many of them in winter that I thought many times if I ever got away from beans I would never eat another one in my life. I never remember a lunch or dinner in our home without them. But, today I love green beans. It's one of my favorite foods, and no one could prepare them quite like Mom could.

Mom was not afraid of the coming of snow and, in the same way, she was not afraid of the coming winter of her own life. Her confidence was not in Daddy, because he couldn't take care of her anymore. Her confidence was in Jesus, and with His help, she took care of her household.

Mom never had finery. For instance, she never had a silk garment. In many ways, she was very plain, but to me she was wonderfully beautiful. I can never forget that she loved the color blue.

Mom was also a woman of very few words. She never listened to gossip, and she never gossiped herself. Much like she did with us when we tried to complain about our father, if we came to her and said something about someone else, she would simply say, "You haven't walked in their shoes, so until you have walked in their shoes, you don't have anything to say about them." And that would be the end of the conversation. You haven't walked in their shoes! PERIOD!

All of us are indebted to my sister Louise because she took Mom in and cared for her for twenty-two years. She did the same thing for her husband's mother and father when they were ill. Louise reached out in a way that the rest of us couldn't reach out and helped in a way that we couldn't help. And the wonderful thing was that she counted it a privilege and an honor.

At one point, Mom had to be placed in a nursing home because her health had deteriorated to the point that she needed way too much care. For two and a half years, she sat in a wheelchair in that stupor, staring at nothing, and we couldn't seem to reach her. This tore our hearts out.

A Foretaste of Glory Divine

None of us could figure out what was wrong with Mom. Was she angry with us because she was in that nursing home and so she was tuning us out? None of us were happy that she was there, but it was because she required constant around-the-clock care. She couldn't feed herself. In fact, she couldn't do anything for herself. She just sat there.

I took some time off from camp and went to visit Mom, staying with my brother James. Each morning I went to the home in time to feed Mom the noonday meal. Then I want back to James' house, and he sometimes would accompany me in the afternoon. We always tried to get there in time to feed Mom her evening meal.

One morning, after about three weeks of this going back and forth, I was driving on Highway 27 and suddenly found myself singing a special song the Lord had placed in my heart. God can give us a song when we don't feel much like singing. As I sang that wonderful song to the Lord, I heard a voice, just as clear as my own, saying, "What are you singing about? Your mom can't even talk to you."

I thought for a moment, "Well, that's true."

I went on down the road, and I started singing again, but then the thought came, "What am I singing about?"

It took me a while to realize that God was trying to give me victory, and, at the same time, the enemy was trying to take it away from me. I can't remember the words of the song, but it was something along the lines that God would never fail; He is always there.

As I sang, I thought about my mom being confined in that wheelchair in that deplorable condition, and God spoke to me and said, "It's the medicine."

I thought, "Wow, it's the medicine!"

When I got to the nursing home, I asked to speak with someone about Mom's medications and was told that there was no one there right then with whom I could talk. I went back that night and stayed until her nurse came. I asked her if mom might be taking some sort of medication that was causing her to sit this way in a stupor.

She said, "Well, maybe. She's taking two different medications that do sometimes cause it."

The next day I called Mom's doctor and talked with him about it, and he assured me that she could not live without those particular medications. If he took her off of them, she would die.

We all talked it over and made a decision that we would rather have our mother living than dead, so it seemed that we had no choice but to leave her on the medications in question.

Then I went on that trip to Poland, and the enemy tormented me with thoughts of my mothers suffering. That was soon to come to a head.

A Foretaste of Glory Divine

Mom was transferred to another facility nearer to James' house, and Louise, too, was able to see her more. Louise is not nearly as mellow as I, and she was not very happy, to say the least, when she learned that they had been bringing Mom's food to her, but no one had been taking the time to feed it to her, and she'd had to be rushed to the hospital suffering from malnutrition. It was reported that this had happened with several other patients in that home.

While Louise was with Mom at the hospital, her doctor came by and said something that lit my sister's fuse. He suggested that we might want to "just let nature take its course" with Mom, meaning not to feed her and let her die. That was a BIG mistake.

Louise grabbed that doctor by the necktie and gave him a good jerk. She said to him, "Look into my eyes. My mother never let a stray dog go hungry in her life, and you are suggesting that we just let her starve to death? You are not her doctor any longer. This is the end of it; you are finished."

The man had been Mother's doctor for fifty years, so this was a big change, but through all of this, God did a miracle. The doctor's associate now took on Mom's case, and he decided to take her off of all those medications. She did not die. Instead, she regained her strength and vitality. She walked again, she talked again, and she sang again, not only for a few days or months, but for the next five years. If that crisis had not happened, Mom would probably have sat there until she went on to be with the Lord. How wonderful that in the midst of it all, God gave me peace about my mom being in a wheelchair. He had a plan.

Mom lived to be eighty-five, and when she passed away, she was just as sweet and wonderful as she had always been. She did not complain even one time about anything that had happened to her. At one point, we'd had to grind her food and then feed it to her like baby food. She remembered even that period as being wonderful, and she sang through it all, never losing sight of God's Blessed Assurance.

God Is Our Strength

ONE OF THE WORST, MOST selfish things I ever did in my life occurred when Dad passed away. I was only in my twenties, and I knew that if Mom cried, I would cry too. If she fell apart, I would fall apart too, and I didn't want that to happen.

I was in the room with Dad when he passed away. Mom came in, and I could see that she was weeping. As she went out, I walked down the hall with her, put my arm around her, and said, "Now, Momma, you know you can't cry. You've got to be strong." I was only saying it because I knew that if she was strong, I could be strong too, but if she wasn't, I couldn't be either.

For that purely selfish motive, I asked my mother not to weep at Dad's funeral, and from that day on, I never saw her weep again. Never!

When Brother Wallace Heflin passed away and went to be with the Lord, God released me from that foolish concept. I was alone on a plane on my way back home to camp the night I had learned about his passing, and I was thinking about us having to be strong and how we could do it, when suddenly I had a vision of Mom in her moment of grief and how selfish I had been. God spoke to me in that moment and said, "You don't have to be strong. I will be your strength," and with those words, He took away all of that need for human effort to be strong. He would be my strength.

In that wonderful way, God released me from that thing I had carried for so many years. I had never been able to go to Mom and say, "I'm sorry that I was so selfish," but now God had released me from it.

Another wonderful thing happened that same night. Like many others, I was personally devastated by our leader's sudden and unexpected death. He had been like a father to me. He was so powerful and commanding that he had constantly inspired each of us to higher heights. Now he was gone.

And now that he was gone, who could possibly hold the large worldwide ministry of Calvary Campground together? It just didn't seem possible. And what did that mean for me personally? I had made that my home for so many years now. Where would we all go? What would we all do?

A Foretaste of Glory Divine

Even as all of this was weighing heavily upon my spirit, a little song began to bubble up in me: *"I will arise and go forth in the name of the Lord, for He has conquered every foe by His name."* It was a song of victory, and even though it was not easy to sing in that moment, I insisted.

As I began to sing that song, I was conflicted. God had been so good to me that I dared not doubt His goodness, and yet my soul was in such agony of grief and loss. I felt shaken. Our pastor was gone, dead. What did the future hold for any of us now?

But as I continued to sing the song, hope began to arise in my heart. I suddenly knew that everything was going to be all right. In those moments, God spoke to me and said, "Yes, he's dead, but I'm not. I'm alive, the vision is still alive, and it will go on."

And it did go on. Sister Ruth Heflin came home from Jerusalem and took the reigns of the ministry, and it thrived under her leadership for the next four years. Then, in 2001, she, too, went to be with the Lord. With the passing of the last remaining member of the Heflin family, I, humble Jane Lowder, from the back country of North Carolina, was now appointed head over this worldwide ministry. What a miracle!

As I think about it now, so many years later, I realize how much that little song God gave me on the plane that night was like another familiar song. I can somehow hear my mother's voice singing in the early morning darkness of a humble country cabin: "Blessed assurance, Jesus is mine. Oh, what a foretaste of glory divine!"

HIGH and LIFTED UP

How Seeing Jesus Propelled
a Sharecropper's Daughter
Into Worldwide Evangelism

Jane Lowder

High and Lifted Up 978-1-58158-050-1

Books by
Ruth Ward Heflin

Glory — 978-1-884369-00-1

Revival Glory — 978-1-884369-80-3

River Glory — 978-1-884369-87-2

Revelation Glory — 978-1-58158-010-5

Golden Glory — 978-1-58158-001-3

Unifying Glory — 978-1-58158-006-8

Harvest Glory — 978-1-884369-81-0

Jerusalem, Zion, Israel and the Nations — 978-1-884369-65-0

Ask for them at your favorite bookstore or from:

Calvary Books

11352 Heflin Lane
Ashland, VA 23005
(804) 798-7756
www.calvarycampground.org

Books by
Rev. Wallace H. Heflin, Jr.

The Power of Prophecy   978-1-884369-22-3
Hear the Voice of God   978-1-884369-36-0
A Pocket Full of Miracles   978-0-914903-23-9
The Bride   978-1-884369-10-0
Jacob and Esau   978-1-884369-01-8
The Potter's House   978-1-884369-61-2
Power in Your Hand   978-1-884369-60-5
Power in Your Hand (Spanish Edition)
         978-1-884369-04-9
The Potter's House (Spanish Edition)
         978-1-58158-035-8
Living By Faith   978-1-58158-113-3

Ask for them at your favorite bookstore or from:

Calvary Books
11352 Heflin Lane
Ashland, VA 23005
(804) 798-7756
www.calvarycampground.org

Calvary Pentecostal Tabernacle

11352 Heflin Lane
Ashland, VA 23005

Tel. (804) 798-7756
Fax (804) 752-2163
www.calvarycampground.org

9 ½ Weeks of Summer Campmeeting
End of June through Labor Day
With two great services daily, 11 A.M. & 7:30 P.M.

Winter Campmeeting
Three Weeks During Winter
Call for details and for room availability

Come and experience the glory with special speakers from around the world.

Revival Meetings
Each Friday night, Saturday morning, Saturday night and Sunday night in all other months

Ministry CDs and DVDs and song CDs are also available upon request.